THE

SENIORS' GUIDE TO THE *BEST*

DEALS, BARGAINS, AND STEALS

The Seniors' Guide to the Best Deals, Bargains, and Steals

with Offers on Retirement Resources, Travel, Recreation, and More!

By the Editors of *Freebies* Magazine

Lowell House
Los Angeles

Contemporary Books
Chicago

Requests for such permissions should be addressed to:

Lowell House
2029 Century Park East, Suite 3290
Los Angeles, CA 90067

Lowell House books can be purchased at special discounts when
ordered in bulk for premiums and special sales. Contact Department JH
at the address above.

Publisher: Jack Artenstein
General Manager, Lowell House Adult: Bud Sperry
Managing Editor: Maria Magallanes
Text design: Laurie Young

ISBN: 1-56565-452-8
Library of Congress Catalog Card Number is available.

Manufactured in the United States of America

10 9 8 7 6 5 4 3 2 1

ACKNOWLEDGMENTS

Few books of this nature come together without the help of talented and dedicated people working together. The Author gratefully acknowledges the commitment of RGA/Lowell House to this project. A special thanks must go to Maria Magallanes and Laurie Young. Their support was a major factor in bringing this book to fruition.

Thanks to Courtney West. A special thanks must also go to Ellen Moggia for her research and writing.

Thanks also to Stephanie O'Donnell for her research and contributions.

Special mention is accorded to Jeff Girod. He gave the extra effort and push that a project like this requires.

ABOUT THIS BOOK

This book is divided into four sections: Financial Planning, Medical, Travel, and General Offers. Each section contains helpful tips, resources, and money-saving offers, as well as general information in an effort to assist you in getting the most out of your golden years. Although great care has been taken in the research and preparation of this material, the author is not in the business of giving specific financial, legal, or other professional advice as it pertains to your particular situation. Before making any decisions that may greatly affect your physical or financial well-being, you should check with your accountant, lawyer, doctor, or other professional in the field who have knowledge of your affairs. The material presented has been confirmed to the best of our ability, but some dates or addresses may have changed since this book's printing. Double-check whenever possible by calling the phone numbers provided.

CONTENTS

TRAVEL AND LEISURE

GENERAL OFFERS

INDEX

PLANNING YOUR RETIREMENT

If you are like most people who are approaching retirement, you are probably concerned about how you will support yourself after you retire. However, before you begin to worry about how much money you will need, figure out what your expenses will be. Today, most people spend twenty years or more in retirement, and they certainly don't spend much of it in a rocking chair. You are entering a new phase of your life, and you can decide how you want to live it.

DETERMINING YOUR NEEDS

Are you happy where you live now? Would you like to live in a smaller home? A bigger home? What about your neighborhood? Would living in a bigger city or a smaller town appeal to you? What about living closer to family and friends? Would you like to reside in a retirement community? What about travel? What places have you always wanted to visit?

Also, how are you going to spend your time? Does volunteer work or a part-time job appeal to you? Would you consider going back to school?

The available opportunities are endless. To make the choices easier, set up three categories—**housing, leisure/work, relationships**—that will help you to sort out your priorities. When you need help making a decision in one of these three areas, the following five-step process is a good model to follow:

1. Define the category or problem that you need to address.
2. Gather information about the problem or challenge.
3. Come up with a probable solution.
4. Test your solution by talking to others and try to imagine all possible consequences, both good and bad, from making that move.
5. Review all your suggestions and choose the one that best fits your future plans and needs.

When changes occur, or when the solution you choose does not seem to work, go back to step two and try again. Keep in mind that it is advisable to have two plans, a short-term plan and a long-term plan, for reaching your retirement goals.

DETERMINING YOUR NET WORTH

Once you have determined how you would like to spend your golden years, you will have to figure out how to budget for them. To support yourself in the manner to which you have become accustomed, you will need to have about two-thirds of your pre-retirement income. To help you plan your savings, you need to determine how much you are now spending, and a quick way to do so is to examine your checkbook.

During your retirement you can plan on spending less on these items: work-related costs, payments to retirement plans, and federal and state income taxes. However, you will probably be spending more on health care and recreational expenses. And don't forget about inflation!

To get a better idea of your future financial status, calculate your *net worth*. Your net worth will provide you with a base point for projecting what your retirement lifestyle will be. To determine your net worth, simply subtract the total amount of your liabilities (what you owe) from the total value of all your assets (what you own).

Assets

When calculating your assets, be sure not to leave out anything. Here is a list of items you may want to include:

Insurance—list all the policies you own, along with their types and any cash values.

Securities—list all the stocks, bonds, and similar items you own, how many shares you own, and their current value.

Bank Accounts—make a note of the account types (certificate of deposit, regular passbook) and values.

Mutual Funds—list the current values and quantities of shares you own.

Real Estate—list the market value of any property you own, and if you own any rental property, list the yearly rental income. List the costs of upkeep and mortgages (if any).

Personal Property—for example, your boat, car, jewelry, and furniture. Be careful not to overestimate the value for sentimental reasons.

Deferred Income—IRAs, pension plans, annuities, and so forth. List the asset types and values. Remember, once you cash these assets in, you will probably need to pay taxes on them.

Collections—stamps, art, even baseball cards. Describe the items and list their appraised value.

Other Assets—any asset not included in the above.

As you document your assets, keep these hints in mind:

1. Round the value up to the nearest $100. Don't forget that stocks and bonds will vary with the market.
2. Take the lower value of an object. Do not be sentimental; use the market price you could get for the item if you had to sell it, not what it would cost you to replace.
3. If you are married, decide if it would be more advantageous to calculate your net worth and your spouse's together or separately.

Liabilities

When you have totaled all your assets, go through your yearly expenses (liabilities). This is the area in which you list all the money you owe. Try to be complete, even down to the amounts you expect to spend on gifts or on your pet. Include your mortgage payments, food allotment, charge accounts, and any other current bills due.

FUTURE SAVINGS

To estimate how much you can add to your savings before retirement, take how much you spend in a year and subtract that from the total income you receive in a year. This procedure tells you what your savings or "dis-savings" will be. A dis-savings occurs when your expenses exceed your income. If this is what you find, correct it quickly! See what you can eliminate from your budget.

Six Simple Steps to Boost Income

1. Call around and find out which bank offers the highest interest on passbook accounts. Many banks offer special accounts to people over 50.
2. Look into a Short-Term Bond Fund. They tend to yield higher percentages than other investments, but they also are subject to unsettling share-price fluctuations.
3. Get rid of high-cost bond and money-market funds that have expensive annual fees.
4. Buy individual high-quality bonds and hold them to maturity. You'll know exactly how much the bonds pay each year and how much you will receive when they mature.

5. While your income is lower, you may wish to buy taxable bonds and pay the taxes.

6. Fight inflation by reinvesting the money you earn through investments to keep your portfolio continually growing. Put some money in stocks to help your portfolio grow.

PENSION HELP

If you are close to retirement, chances are you are spending a great deal of time figuring out your financial stability for the years you will no longer receive a paycheck. Many people will rely on their company pension as a major source of income. However, you should research the conditions of the pension and possibly seek financial assistance. Listed below are some resources to help you make sure you collect everything to which you are entitled.

- The Labor Department's Pension and Welfare Benefits Administration (check your phone book)

- The Pension Rights Center has a national lawyer referral service for those who need legal aid regarding pension issues. For more information, write to:

> PENSION RIGHTS CENTER,
> 918 16th St., NW, Suite 704
> Washington, DC 20006

- Some states offer specific help:
  Arizona: (602) 790-7267

California:
    San Francisco Bay area (415) 474-5171
    All other areas 1-800-474-1116

Georgia: 1-800-669-8387

Massachusetts:
    Boston area (617) 287-7311
    All other areas 1-800-882-2003

Michigan:
    Greater Detroit area (810) 262-9218
    Upper Peninsula area (906) 786-4701

Minnesota:
    Twin Cities area (612) 645-0261
    All other areas 1-800-365-8765

Missouri:
    St. Louis area (314) 997-1811

New York:
    New York City area (212) 997-7714
    All other areas 1-800-414-7714

INVESTMENTS

If you decide to try to add to your net worth, it would be wise to take a look at your investment opportunities. But before you invest, consider the following questions so that you will be better prepared to choose your investment. Given your age (and your health), would long-term or short-term investments be more practical? Also, how much time do you have until you retire? How much money do you have available to invest? Is there enough in the bank for emergencies? Do you have loans that you need to repay? What about your children's education? Finally, ask yourself about the risk. How comfortable are you with taking chances? Your age and financial situation should have a bearing on how much risk you are willing to take.

Risk Factor

The risk factor in investments ranges from high to minimal:

High Risk—These have a significant growth potential, but there is also a chance that you can lose your principal and earnings.

- *commodities; precious metals; options; nonrated (junk) bonds; aggressive growth stocks*

Moderate Risk—These offer an increased growth or income potential, but you may lose some of the principal.

- *blue-chip stocks and mutual funds; investment-grade corporate bonds and funds; investment-grade municipal bonds and funds; utilities*

Low Risk—These present a good possibility of increased income, with a minimal potential of loss of principal.

- *U.S. direct obligations (over one year); U.S. agency obligations and mutual funds (over one year); high-grade municipal bonds and funds; protected tax-deferred insurance contracts (annuities); certificates of deposit (over one year)*

Minimal Risk—These are protected investments and, although they offer a high degree of safety, their up-side potential is limited.

- *federally insured investments; passbook savings; certificates of deposit (one year or less); bank or government or municipal money-market instruments or mutual funds; U.S. government direct obligations (one year or less)*

Economic trends and conditions can also put your investments at risk.

Inflation Risk—Rising prices reduce the purchasing power of an investment. Rising inflation erodes the value of future income on investments with fixed payments, long-term bonds in particular.

Interest-Rate Risk—Rising interest rates cause investments to drop in price. Investing borrowed money in margin accounts or through floating-rate debt increases the interest-rate risk.

Economic Risk—Slower growth in the economy causes investments to fall in price.

Market Risk—Market risk includes such factors as political developments and Wall Street fads. For example, gold carries market risk because its price moves sharply when a political or military upheaval in another country encourages the flight of capital.

Specific Risk—Some investments carry specific risks that are unique to a single firm or industry. For example, technology stocks (or other areas) may not act in concert with a rising trend in the market as a whole. They often respond to specific events within that industry in spite of other economic indicators.

Also, consider whether the potential investment is tax-free or tax-deferred; some investments offer the added benefit of tax-deferred earnings, making the investment an excellent choice for your retirement portfolio. The earnings from these investments only become taxable when you withdraw the funds. While the money is in the bank accumulating interest, you do not have to pay taxes on your investment. Tax-free investment earnings are often completely exempt from taxes (federal and/or state), and thus their stated yield will probably be lower than taxable investments. To decide on the best investment, be sure you consider the after-tax earnings when comparing tax-free or tax-deferred to taxable investments.

Making Your Investment Decision

Start by asking yourself:

1. How much risk am I willing to take?
2. Am I planning to invest for a short time or for the long term?
3. What do I want out of my investment? For example, do I want an investment that will give a steady source of income each month after I retire or one that looks for growth?
4. Do I need a product to help me start saving for a particular goal? Can I put aside a certain amount each month for an investment that will grow over time?
5. How does my tax bracket affect my investment decisions? Do I need an investment that will allow me to defer taxes until a later date?

Seven Common Investing Mistakes

1. Keeping too much money in any one company's fund or stock.
2. Leaving too much money in cash. This offers you no chance for capital gains that can outpace rising prices.

3. Assembling your portfolio piecemeal. A collection of great individual investments doesn't always give your portfolio the balance it needs.
4. Buying more investments than you can monitor.
5. Focusing too narrowly in any one sector.
6. Not keeping yourself abreast of your investments and their current status.
7. Not seeking advice if you have questions.

Where to Get Advice

If you don't know someone to turn to for advice, or to answer any questions, the organizations listed below can refer you to financial planners in your area.

INTERNATIONAL ASSOCIATION FOR FINANCIAL PLANNING
Two Concourse Pkwy.
Suite 800
Atlanta, GA 30328
(404) 395-1605

NATIONAL ASSOCIATION OF PERSONAL FINANCIAL ADVISORS
1130 Lake Cook Rd.
Suite 150
Buffalo Grove, IL 60089
1-800-366-2732; (708) 537-7722

INSTITUTE OF CERTIFIED FINANCIAL PLANNERS
7600 E. Eastman Ave.
Suite 301
Denver, CO 80231
1-800-282-7526

AMERICAN ASSOCIATION OF INDIVIDUAL INVESTORS
625 N. Michigan Ave.
Suite 1900
Chicago, IL 60611
(312) 280-0170

REVERSE MORTGAGES

If, after calculating your net worth, investments, and future expenses, you feel that you will need more money to retire comfortably, a *Reverse Mortgage* might be right for you. A reverse mortgage takes the house you have worked so hard to own and makes your investment work for you. The Reverse Mortgage is a way to get money from your house without selling it. It is a tax-free loan that the lender will pay to you either in monthly installments or as a direct line of credit, allowing you to access the amount of money as you need it.

After a slow start in the early 1990s, Reverse Mortgages are getting a boost from financial services companies and are becoming more widely known and used. The American Association of Retired Persons (AARP) calls the Reverse Mortgage concept "one of the most significant financial tools" available to older homeowners in the 1990s.

Unlike other loans, a Reverse Mortgage does not require you to repay the loan immediately. Depending on the type of Reverse Mortgage you choose, payment will not be due until you sell the house, until you die, or until the time specified in the agreement.

As with any loan decision, it would be best to consult your financial adviser or attorney before taking out a Reverse Mortgage.

Setup Costs

Reverse Mortgages are not free. There is a setup fee, usually around $3,000, plus a charge of 7 percent of the house's appraisal value, including interest.

There are two ways to go about paying the setup fees of a Reverse Mortgage. One way is to go through a lender who will share in the home's future appreciation value. In this case, the setup fees may be lower than those of a lender who does not take part in the home's future value. However, not only will you have to repay all of the stipends (monthly amounts of money you receive) plus interest, you will have to pay the lender a percent of your home's new value. The way to avoid future costs is to pay the higher setup fees up front.

When you are trying to decide which option to choose, keep in mind your future plans. If you intend to move, or if the prices of the homes in your neighborhood are basically staying the same, you should probably choose the lower setup cost. Alternately, if you intend to continue living in your home and/or the prices of homes in your area are rising, you might choose the higher cost option.

Types of Loans

There are three types of loans: *tenure, term,* and *line of credit.* How much you can borrow depends on the value of your home, the amount of equity in it, and your age. A lender will use the statistical average life span (for women it is 79 years; for men it is 72 years) to determine how much money you can borrow. The older you are, the more money you can receive each month.

Tenure Loan—This guarantees that you will continue receiving monthly stipends for as long as you live in the house. If you die, your estate will then repay the money.

Term Loan—This is a monthly stipend paid only for a specified period of time (usually 5 to 12 years). After the time period, the borrower must repay the money, with interest, in a lump sum.

Line of Credit—This sets you up with a sum of money available for your withdrawal whenever you need it. You can take as much or as little as you need, and you repay only what you use.

Portable Lifetimer Reverse Mortgage—This is another type of loan that is usually difficult to find. Ask about this arrangement when you seek advice about reverse mortgages.

Non-recourse Loan—This is important to have. This means that the lender cannot take more than the house is worth. For example, if your house was appraised at a certain value but sold for less, you would need to make up the difference to the lender unless you had a non-recourse loan.

Also, in obtaining a loan, you will need to choose between a *fixed-rate* loan and an *adjustable rate* loan. With a fixed-rate loan, you will have the security that your interest rate will never change. An adjustable rate follows the market, and the homeowner stands to gain only if financial costs decline.

FHA Reverse Mortgages

For added security, you may want to obtain your Reverse Mortgage through the *Federal Housing Authority (FHA) program* and thus acquire government insurance on the loan.

This added insurance often prompts lenders to lower their interest rates and setup fees. It also allows you to "mix and match" the different types of loans. For example, you could receive a monthly stipend but have a backup line of credit just in case. Plus, you don't have to repay an FHA loan when the term of the loan expires. The stipends you receive will stop, but it will not be necessary to repay the money until you sell the house or die. As of this writing, the FHA received congressional authorization to insure up to 25,000 Reverse Mortgages.

One disadvantage to the FHA program is that federal law prohibits the agency from insuring a loan of more than $124,950. Also, if you deplete your credit line, there is no way to borrow any more cash to meet an emergency cash need.

Is a Reverse Mortgage Right for You?

If a Reverse Mortgage sounds like the opportunity you have been looking for, great! But before you rush into anything, take a few minutes to answer these questions:

1. Are you in poor health? If so, you probably will not be able to enjoy all the benefits of a Reverse Mortgage.
2. Are you planning to move? If you sign up for a Reverse Mortgage, will you be able to afford another place to live and make the payments on that loan, too? Remember, once you sell the house, the loan is due.
3. Do you want to leave the house to your heirs? If you have a Reverse Mortgage, there is a chance that your heirs may need to forfeit your house to repay the loan.

Here are two alternatives to a Reverse Mortgage.

Sale/Lease Back of Your House— This allows you to sell the house to your child and simultaneously sign a lease saying that you may rent the house as long as you wish. With this option, you can live off the resale profits and still pass your home through the family. Also, there is a special law that makes seniors eligible for a one time only, $125,000 tax-free exclusion from the sale of their home.

Home Equity Loan—This allows you to borrow against the equity in your home. This is the difference between the balance of your mortgage and the current market value of your house. Home equity loans offer a revolving line of credit, and you pay interest only on the amount you use. Also, interest on the first $100,000 of your home equity loan is currently tax deductible. However, your home is the collateral, and the monthly loan payments and closing costs may be a problem for you if you are living on a fixed income.

Whatever you decide to do, your best bet is to talk with a certified financial planner and/or lawyer first. The planner may help you find a less expensive way to solve your financial problems. The lawyer will make sure that you—and not just the lender—are protected in the reverse mortgage.

For more information, send a postcard requesting *Homemade Money: A Consumer's Guide to Home Equity Conversion* and a list of Reverse Mortgage lenders to:

> AARP
> HOME EQUITY INFORMATION CENTER
> CONSUMER AFFAIRS
> 601 E St. NW
> Washington, DC 20049

For a list of all public and private sources in the United States, send $1 and a self-addressed, stamped business-size envelope to the following address, and the center will send you its "Reverse Mortgage Locator":

NATIONAL CENTER FOR HOME EQUITY CONVERSION
7373 147th St. West
Apple Valley, MN 55124

Six Tips About Reverse Mortgages

1. The amount of money you can receive depends on your age and value of your home. Usually, the older you are and the higher the value of your home, the more you can borrow.
2. Contact a lender and find out the amount you are eligible for and how it can be paid. Usually it's a monthly payment, but it can also be a lump sum, a line of credit, or a combination of payment types.
3. Consider whether you want to retain some equity in your home.
4. Consider the costs involved with the transaction. As with any type of loan, some institutions have higher fees than others.
5. Review the documents with your financial adviser or attorney before signing.
6. Funds received are loans and are not treated as income for tax purposes.

LIVING TRUSTS

Another aspect of retirement that you should consider is establishing a revocable Living Trust and/or a Living Will. A revocable Living Trust contains all of your assets. You act as your own Trustee and decide how the assets in the Living Trust (your assets) are managed and how distributions are made. Since the Living Trust is revocable, you can change it as your personal situation changes. A nonrevocable Living Trust is just that—once the trust has begun, it is permanent and changes are not permitted.

A Living Will allows you to provide instructions for future medical decisions that you may not be capable of making in the future. You can indicate, for example, whether you want to be kept alive by use of a respirator or mechanical ventilator, or by the use of a feeding tube or invasive surgery. The Living Will will document and record your medical treatment decisions in the event you cannot voice them for yourself.

A Living Trust is a common legal choice used in planning for retirement. It authorizes a person other than you to handle and deal with your assets. A Living Trust can also buy, sell, or own property, manage property and other assets, and spend money to accommodate your regular living expenses. A revocable Living Trust may be changed, altered, or even dissolved as your situation changes.

A Living Trust can save your estate thousands of dollars because probate and legal fees are eliminated. Upon your passing, the Living Trust passes your assets to whomever you name as co-trustee.

The Living Trust can also be used if you become incapacitated. The co-trustee, or successor trustee, can act for you without the expense and aggravation of legal and court action. The Living Trust can also pass money, without court action, to beneficiaries that you name.

To set up your revocable Living Trust you will need:

1. At least one or more beneficiaries.
2. A trustee (usually yourself) and a co-trustee or successor trustee.
3. Physical assets to be contributed in the name of the trust (house, money, stocks/bonds, life insurance, etc.).
4. A documented revocable Living Trust that spells out your wishes to the co-trustee or successor trustee.

Check with your lawyer and accountant for advice in setting up your revocable Living Trust.

When you set up your revocable Living Trust, you may be the lifetime beneficiary, and you can also list others. Your revocable Living Trust can also indicate to whom the property of the trust should go when you pass on. In a sense, the revocable Living Trust can almost act as a will.

A trustee can be anyone you choose (for instance, your spouse, a trusted friend, or your lawyer in the trust department of your bank).

The physical assets that are contributed to the trust are whatever assets you choose to contribute. You do not have to place all of your assets into the revocable Living Trust.

Disadvantages of a Living Trust

Although there are advantages to a revocable Living Trust, you should also realize that there are disadvantages to this procedure.

The major disadvantage is the setup cost. The contribution of the physical assets often requires paperwork that allows the assets to be placed in trust. As you have probably guessed, paperwork is time consuming and expensive. Plus, the lawyer or accountant who helps with the development of your revocable Living Trust will charge a fee.

Other disadvantages to consider in a revocable Living Trust is that your bank may have minimum trust values that they will accept. (The minimum may be $100,000 or more.) You should check with your bank on its minimum levels of acceptance.

Your revocable Living Trust will also need a friend or family member who is willing and capable of accepting the job of trustee or successor for little or no pay. Also, the revocable Living Trust will not eliminate your need for a will or power of attorney. A revocable Living Trust can, however, make drawing up these documents less cumbersome.

As you think about and plan your golden years of retirement, you need to think about your personal situation and whether a revocable Living Trust is beneficial for you. Talk to your spouse, your lawyer, and your accountant to determine the advantages and disadvantages of a revocable Living Trust.

ADVANCE MEDICAL DIRECTIVES

Who makes decisions for you when you're too sick to make your own? What if you are involved in an accident or suffer a stroke and cannot speak for yourself? Will your spouse, family, or doctor know what your wishes are?

Advance Directives (the general term for Living Wills and Durable Powers of Attorney) are documents that you fill out today to ensure that your choices regarding medical treatment are followed.

The late Jacqueline Kennedy Onassis and former president Richard Nixon had something in common: They signed Living Wills, legal documents that spell out medical treatments to accept or refuse at the end of life.

As a result of Mrs. Onassis's and Mr. Nixon's decision to make explicit wishes known in a Living Will, a surge of public interest and demand for Living Wills and other advance directives was reported.

All fifty states and the District of Columbia have laws recognizing some form of advance directive—either a Living Will or a Durable Power of Attorney for health care ("health care proxy"). Living Wills are signed, legal written instructions that explain an individual's wishes regarding end-of-life medical treatment, including life support. A health care proxy is used to appoint someone else to make health care decisions in the event that the individual is unable to communicate.

According to Dr. Karen Orloff Kaplan, executive director of Choice in Dying, the nation's largest distributor of state-specific advance directives, "Many people don't know how to make the difficult decisions involved with Living Wills. It's important to discuss medical wishes with family, friends, and medical professionals."

Dr. Kaplan explained that laws authorizing Living Wills vary from state to state. Preparing the form is not difficult and does not require a lawyer. However, you must ensure that the advance directive conforms with state law.

Choice in Dying has trained staff that can answer questions about advance directives and state law. They also provide information to families struggling with end-of-life medical treatment decisions.

For free, preprinted, state-specific forms, write to:

CHOICE IN DYING
200 Varick St.
New York, NY 10014-4810
1-800-989-WILL; (212) 366-5540

In considering your Living Will, you must be careful in your definitions and choices. Don't just say "I do/do not want extraordinary care." Clearly define what you mean by "extraordinary care." For example:

1. I refuse/I want to have a respirator or mechanical ventilator to be used in my medical care.
2. I do/do not want to be fed via an artificial feeding tube.
3. I do/do not want radiotherapy, chemotherapy, or antibiotic therapy to be used in my medical care.
4. I do/do not want invasive (aggressive) surgical techniques to be used in my medical care.

You can amend your American Medical Directives at any time you want. Changing it is as simple as changing any will. You can add or delete instructions, add a codicil, or cancel it entirely.

The preparation and execution of your Advance Medical Directive is a serious procedure and many people are not comfortable in discussing it. Your Living Will affords you the opportunity to express and protect your desires about your future medical care.

A new type of Living Will is available from Harvard Medical School's *Health Letter*. It's called the "Medical Directive" and is sure to cover most questions you may have about Living Wills.

The Medical Directive lists twelve standard medical procedures or treatments, ranging from pain medication to cardiopulmonary resuscitation. For each situation, there is a place for you to indicate whether you would want medical intervention that might prolong your life. This Medical Directive includes a proxy form so you can designate someone you trust to make these difficult decisions when you can no longer do so. It also includes a form enabling you to become an organ donor.

When you and two witnesses sign and date the Medical Directive, it provides legal support for your doctor to carry out your intentions. Check with your attorney general's office to see if the Medical Directive is considered a legal document in your state.

Because this form is new, your doctor may not be familiar with it. Bring it to your next appointment and discuss it. After the directive has been completed and signed, your doctor should have a copy. You also should give a copy to the person whom you expect to be closest should you become ill.

If you want copies of this form, send a check or money order to:

MEDICAL DIRECTIVE
P.O. Box 6100
Holliston, MA 01746-6100

The cost is two copies for $6 or five copies for $11 (includes postage and handling). This could be the most important investment you will ever make.

SAMPLE LIVING WILL

Living Will Declaration

To my Family, Doctors, and All Those Concerned with My Care

I,_____, being of sound mind, make this statement as a directive to be followed if I become unable to participate in decisions regarding my medical care.

If I should be in an incurable or irreversible mental or physical condition with no reasonable expectation of recovery, I direct my attending physician to withhold or withdraw treatment that merely prolongs my dying. I further direct that treatment be limited to measures to keep me comfortable and to relieve pain.

These directions express my legal right to refuse treatment. Therefore I expect my family, doctors, and everyone concerned with my care to regard themselves as legally and morally bound to act in accord with my wishes, and in so doing to be free of any legal liability for having followed my directions.

I especially do not want: (for example: cardiac resuscitation, artificial feeding tubes, invasive surgery)

Other instructions/comments: (for example: I do/do not want medication for pain or I do/do not want to die at home)

Proxy Designation Clause: Should I become unable to communicate my instructions as stated above, I designate the following person to act in my behalf:

_____
(Name)

_____
(Address)

If the person I have named above is unable to act in my behalf, I authorize the following person to do so:

_____
(Name)

_____
(Address)

Signed: _____

Date: _____

Witness: _____

Witness: _____

SOCIAL SECURITY: AN OVERVIEW

If you are like most people, the government's Social Security program will not concern you until you approach retirement age. However, what many adults fail to realize is that Social Security is much more than a retirement program. Although it is true that most beneficiaries (about 60 percent) are those who receive retirement benefits, Social Security is in fact a broad package of protections. It provides for the disabled; for dependents of those who receive Social Security; and for the widow, widower, or child of someone who has died.

The basic idea behind Social Security is that you pay taxes into the system during your working years, and you and members of your family are eligible to receive monthly benefits when you retire or if you become disabled. The program also provides partial protection against the high cost of health care under Medicare, and your survivors can also collect benefits. Nonetheless, the government never intended Social Security to be your sole source of income. It is intended to serve as a supplement to the insurance, savings, pensions, and other investments you have acquired during your employment years.

Eligibility

Retirees can collect Social Security checks as early as age 62; usually, however, only those who delay drawing Social Security until age 65 receive full benefits. Once you become eligible for Social Security, you will receive benefits related to the age at which you retired and the amount of your earnings over the years.

If you become injured and are unable to work for at least one year, you are eligible for disability benefits. In some cases, when you have received payments for two years, you may be eligible for Medicare even if you are under age 65.

To be eligible for Social Security, a surviving spouse must have been married at least nine months to the covered spouse before the latter's death (unless the death was due to an accident or military duty, or the surviving spouse is the parent of a dependent child). If the surviving spouse is caring for an eligible child under age 16 or a child disabled before age 22, he or she must have been married for one year to that spouse. The surviving spouse is then entitled to 75 percent of the covered spouse's *Primary Insurance Amount (PIA)*.

Credits and Your Primary Insurance Amount

As you work and pay taxes, you accumulate Social Security *credits*. You earn one credit for each $540 of your earnings. Four credits is the maximum that you can earn in one year. Each year the amount of money required to earn one credit increases. Most people need 40 credits (ten years of work) in order to qualify for benefits. The Social Security Administration bases benefits on what it calls the *Primary Insurance Amount (PIA)*. Social Security calculates the PIA according to a formula applied to your lifetime covered earnings. The higher your income and the more taxes you pay, the higher your PIA.

You can obtain an official statement of earnings and your approximate retirement benefits by visiting your local Social Security office and requesting Form SSA-7004. A few weeks after you fill out this questionnaire, you will receive a Personal Earnings and Benefit Estimate Statement. It tells you how much you can expect when you retire and provides estimates of the disability benefits for which you might be eligible and any benefits payable to your family if you should die.

Applying for Social Security Benefits

You must apply for Social Security benefits; they do not come to you automatically at age 65. When you visit your Social Security office to apply, you may need to supply some or all of the following documents, depending on the circumstances of your claim:

- Your Social Security card (or a record of your number)
- Your birth certificate
- Your children's birth certificates (if they are applying)
- Your marriage certificate (if signing up on spouse's record)
- Your most recent W-2 form, or a copy of your federal tax return if you are self-employed

Supplementary Security Income (SSI)

If you do not qualify for Social Security and have had health problems that have limited or depleted your assets, the federal *Supplementary Security Income (SSI)* will provide some benefits. SSI is for people who are 65 or older, blind, or disabled, who have limited income and assets. General revenue funds of the U.S. Treasury (personal income, corporate, and other taxes) finance SSI payments. Although SSI makes monthly payments to people who have few resources and little or no income, you can own a home, car, and personal belongings of reasonable value and still be eligible to receive SSI benefits. The basic monthly SSI check is the same throughout the United States. In 1995, the basic rate will be $434 for one person and $653 for a couple. This amount is reduced if you live rent-free in someone else's home or if the state pays for your room and board at an institution.

Benefits for Your Family

When you begin to collect Social Security disability or retirement benefits, you might not be the only one in your family who is eligible for payments. These other members of your family may also receive benefits:

- Your husband or wife if he or she is 62 or older
- Your husband or wife, at any age, if he or she is caring for your child (the child must be under 16 or disabled)
- Your children, if they are unmarried and
    —under 18;
    —under 19 but in elementary or secondary school as full-time students; or
    —over 18 but severely disabled (the disability must have started before age 22).

Disability Benefits

In order to qualify for disability benefits from Social Security, you must have a physical or mental impairment that is expected to prevent you from performing any "substantial" work for at least one year. If you become disabled, you should file for disability benefits immediately. You can do this by calling or visiting any Social Security office. The staff can process your claim sooner if you have the following medical and vocational information when you apply:

- the names, addresses, and phone numbers of your doctors and of hospitals, clinics, and so forth, where you have been treated;
- a summary of the places you worked in the last 15 years and the kinds of work you did.

If the Social Security office agrees that you are disabled, you will receive monthly benefits beginning with the sixth full month of your disability. The Social Security office may reduce the amount of your benefit if you get worker's compensation or certain other government disability benefits. Your benefits will continue unless your condition improves significantly or you return to work.

Who Gets Survivors Benefits

Nearly 20 percent of the 39 million people receiving Social Security checks also receive Survivors Benefits. Indeed, a portion of the Social Security taxes you pay is allocated to survivors insurance. Currently, 98 out of every 100 children are eligible for benefits if a working parent should die.

You can receive Survivors Benefits only if you have enough PIA credits for work in jobs or self-employment covered by Social Security. However, your children and your spouse can receive benefits even though you may not have the number of PIA credits needed. They are eligible to receive benefits if you have credit for 1.5 years of work in the last 3 years.

If you should die, Social Security Survivors Benefits can go to the following people:

- your widow or widower—full benefits at age 65 or older or reduced benefits as early as age 60. A disabled widow or widower can receive benefits if he or she is between the ages of 50 and 60.
- your widow or widower—at any age if he or she takes care of your child who is under age 16 or disabled and receiving benefits.
- your unmarried children—under age 18 (or under age 19 if they are attending elementary school or secondary school full-time). Your child can receive benefits at any age if he or she was disabled before age 22 and remains disabled. Under certain circumstances, Social Security benefits may also be paid to your grandchildren.
- your dependent parents—at age 62 or older.

Other Benefits

When anyone covered by Social Security dies, the administration makes a lump-sum death payment of $225, payable to a surviving spouse who was living with the deceased at the time of death. If there is no spouse, the lump-sum death payment goes to children who are eligible for benefits in the month of death. Otherwise, there is no payment.

Representative Payees

While most people who receive Social Security payments are able to manage and spend their own money, some are sick or incapable of handling a bank account, paying bills, and making financial decisions. If you are in this situation, you can appoint a *representative payee* to take over your responsibilities. A payee is an individual or an institution (such as a nursing home or mental hospital) that is chosen or appointed to receive Social Security payments on behalf of the beneficiary. Once designated, the payee is the only person (or institution) who has the legal right to spend the beneficiary's money. Under Social Security Administration policy, the person who wants to be considered for the position of payee must complete an application that covers his or her qualifications to be a payee, his or her relationship to the beneficiary, the availability of other potential payees, and how he or she would spend the benefits if appointed payee. The application also requires the potential payee to state that he or she is aware of the penalties for the misuse of funds.

Avoiding Social Security Hustlers

Many retirees fear for the safety of their Social Security benefits. Many hustlers and con artists are well aware of this fear and often take advantage of these concerned seniors. For example, you may receive an official-looking envelope containing a form authorizing an organization to get a statement of your earnings from the Social Security Administration. Perhaps you'll find warnings of a possible end to Social Security and a request for funds to prevent its disappearance.

Don't let yourself be fooled! You can obtain a copy of your Social Security records for free, and you should never trust anyone posing as an official from the Social Security Administration. Contact your local post office or Social Security office if you suspect that something or someone isn't right.

FINANCIAL OFFERS

Budget Booster

SEND:
A long SASE

ASK FOR:
Sample copy of
The Budget Booster

MAIL TO:
Budget Booster
P.O. Box 992
Berwick, ME 03901

The Budget Booster is offering a FREE copy of its newsletter for people who want to minimize wasteful spending and get more out of their money. It's loaded with helpful tips as well as money-saving recipes and craft ideas.

Cutting Costs

SEND:
A long SASE

ASK FOR:
Sample copy of
Skinflint News

MAIL TO:
Skinflint News
P.O. Box 818
Palm Harbor, FL 34682

Learn how to cut back on expenses with a FREE copy of the *Skinflint News*. This nationally circulated monthly newsletter of thrifty advice offers tips for saving time and money in all areas of your life.

A Few Lines to Save You Money

SEND:
Your Name and Address

ASK FOR:
Savvy Discounts Newsletter

MAIL TO:
Savvy Discounts Newsletter P.O. Box 96 Smyrna, NC 28579

Savvy Discounts Newsletter promises to save you at least $840 each and every year you subscribe. This remarkable quarterly shows you how to spend less on almost everything you buy; from little-known secrets that lower your phone bill to getting a bargain on a new car, from luxury vacations at half-price to the best deals in mail order. *Savvy Discounts* is offering a FREE eight-page sample issue. It is chock-full of easy and useful money-saving tips that anyone can use.

How Long Will Your Money Last?

SEND:
A long SASE with two first class stamps affixed

ASK FOR:
"How Long Will My Money Last?"

MAIL TO:
The Financial Training Group 300 East Blvd., B-4 Charlotte, NC 28203

Most people want to retire as early as possible. You may be one of them, but will you have the money to do it and still live the lifestyle you'd like to live? The cost of living is doubling approximately every 18 years, and the average American man and woman are living well into their 80s, even their early 90s.

Now you can find out—at a glance—just how much money

you'll need when you retire with a FREE reference card, "How Long Will My Money Last?"

You'll also receive a FREE copy of the latest issue of *Bill Staton's Money Advisory,* called "America's most user-friendly financial newsletter." It's chock-full of money-making and money-saving ideas—and it's written in plain folk talk, not "Wall Street-ese."

A Penny Earned

SEND:
A long SASE

ASK FOR:
Sample copy of
A Penny Saved

MAIL TO:
A Penny Saved
RR 5, Box 67
Council Bluffs, IA 51503

You're not cheap, you just want to be careful how you spend your hard-earned money. You're just the kind of person who would appreciate a FREE sample issue of *A Penny Saved*. This timely newsletter is designed for middle-class people who are trying to save and spend their money wisely.

The eight-page monthly publication addresses all aspects of financial well-being, including saving money on groceries, tax savings, inexpensive home decorating, and more.

Ready, Set, Retire!

Confusion and apprehension are often the biggest obstacles to a secure retirement, says J. William Brimacombe, author of the book *Ready, Set, Retire!* The book is now being offered FREE by John Hancock Financial Services as part of an effort to educate consumers and help them plan for their retirement. These days, people are living longer, and both employers and the government have started to relinquish their responsibility for retirement funding. As a result, the burden of retirement planning is falling increasingly on the shoulders of the individual.

If you're planning your retirement, this book will show you how to use tax-smart strategies to get there with less pain and less money. If you're already retired, you'll discover tax-smart strategies that can stretch your limited resources to cover your life span. And you'll learn to live with financial peace of mind.

Taxation Information

PHONE:
1-800-336-3063

ASK FOR:
"Nine Tax Tips for Mutual Fund Investors"

For the one in four American households that owns mutual funds, GIT Investment Funds has prepared a FREE pamphlet titled "Nine Tax Tips for Mutual Fund Investors." The pamphlet includes strategies for minimizing capital gains taxation, avoiding double taxation on dividends, and computing cost basis.

Don't wait until April 15 to be at the mercy of the tax man. Be smart and order this pamphlet now.

PAYING FOR
HEALTH CARE

Finding the resources to pay for health care is probably the greatest financial problem facing older Americans. Costs continue to rise at a phenomenal rate each year, and health care spending is at its highest point ever.

Furthermore, senior citizens constitute a huge portion of all medical clientele, and they consume more over-the-counter and prescription drugs than any other segment of the population. The need for regular professional health care is an absolute fact for all but the luckiest and healthiest of America's seniors.

Unfortunately, many people simply cannot afford to pay for the care they need, or they find their lifelong savings and assets quickly depleted by health care bills. Will the government eventually take over all health care matters? Perhaps. One thing is certain, however: It will be years, and maybe decades, before any real changes or improvements in our health care system occurs. In the meantime, paying for health care will probably remain your responsibility. Yes, the Medicare program can help you, but it cannot pay for everything. Be prepared to pay for additional coverage beyond the Medicare basics.

MEDICARE

Dealing with Medicare can seem almost as traumatic as being ill or injured. Indeed, determining which medical fees Medicare will and will not cover can cause major headaches.

This section attempts to simplify and clarify Medicare parameters. However, before we begin, there are two facts you should know: The first is that Medicare does offer many benefits and is an excellent source of health insurance coverage. The second is that Medicare is *not* comprehensive. In other words, Medicare will pay a large portion of your health care bills, but the program will not pay for all of them. In fact, the program's creators did not design it to pay all of the costs associated with an individual's health care. Currently, Medicare pays less than half of the average beneficiary's health care bill.

What Is Medicare?

Run by a federal agency called the Health Care Financing Administration, Medicare is a federal health insurance program for senior citizens (age 65 and over) and certain disabled people. Your local Social Security office takes applications and provides basic information about the program. Typically, though, most Social Security offices are unable to answer specific questions about the program. The best place to get specific information about Medicare is through a local advocate for the elderly. (Look under "Legal Services" or "Commission on Aging" in your phone book, and check the Intermediaries and Carriers lists at the end of this chapter.)

Medicare consists of two parts. Each covers different areas of seniors' health care needs:

Part A—Hospital Insurance, which covers these general areas:

1. Inpatient hospital care
2. Inpatient care in a skilled nursing facility
3. Home health care
4. Hospice care

Part B—Medical Insurance ("the doctor's part"), which covers these general areas:

1. Medically necessary doctor's services
2. Certain therapies
3. Outpatient services
4. Medical equipment
5. Some services not covered by Part A

Remember, even if you are covered by both Part A and Part B, Medicare will not pay all of your expenses. Before either part will pay anything, you or another insurance plan must pay the deductible and co-insurance amounts.

Am I Eligible for Medicare?
How Do I Pay for It?

If you are over 65 and are entitled to Social Security benefits (even if you are not currently receiving them), you automatically qualify for Medicare Part A and will not have to pay anything to receive the benefits. Others may purchase Medicare by paying a monthly premium. (In 1995 the monthly premium was $183 or $261, depending on how many Social Security work credits you or your spouse has).

General taxes fund most of Medicare Part B, but monthly premiums finance 25 percent of the cost. (In 1995 the monthly premium was $46.10.) This amount comes directly out of an individual's Social Security checks. Others receive quarterly billings from the Social Security department.

Called *intermediaries,* private insurance companies have contracts with the government to handle Medicare payments and claims processing for Medicare Part A. The private insurance companies that handle the claims processing and payments for Medicare Part B are called *carriers.*

What Is the Difference Between Medicare
and Medicaid?

Medicaid is a program designed to pay some of the health care costs for people with very low incomes and few assets. The costs paid by Medicaid are ones not already covered by Medicare. The eligibility requirements for Medicaid vary from state to state. Your local Social Security office can tell you what your state's requirements are. If you qualify as a

Medicaid beneficiary, your state medical assistance program will pay your share of health costs under Medicare.

In general, to qualify for Medicaid, you must meet the following requirements:

1. Your annual income must not exceed the national poverty level.
2. You have no access to financial resources such as bank accounts or stocks and bonds.

If you qualify for Medicaid, you will not need any other type of medical insurance because Medicaid will pay the majority of your expenses.

The Medicare "Traps"

There are three specific terms or restrictions that Medicare uses to narrow the types of health care the program will cover: To qualify for Medicare coverage, (1) the health care you receive must be performed by Medicare-certified providers, (2) it must be care that is reasonable and necessary, and (3) it must be skilled care.

Medicare-certified providers are health care organizations and professionals who meet all licensing requirements of state and local health authorities as well as additional Medicare requirements. To verify certification, call the provider or your carrier or intermediary.

In order for care to be considered *reasonable* and *necessary* for the diagnosis or treatment of injury or illness, you must already be sick or injured. The health care you receive must be in response to your injury or illness. Medicare does not cover preventive health care or items such as hearing aids that do not "treat" a condition.

The difference between *skilled care* (which Medicare does cover) and *custodial care* (which Medicare does not cover) may seem slight, but according to Medicare regulations, there is a world of difference. Medicare defines *skilled care* as that which can be provided only by persons with professional health care skills and training. *Custodial care* differs from skilled care in that it is primarily for the purpose of meeting personal needs and can be provided by people who are not professionally trained.

Part A—The Hospital Part

If you meet all of the coverage criteria, Medicare Part A covers these four areas of your health care:

1. Periods of severe illness or injury that require inpatient hospitalization
2. Care in a skilled nursing home
3. Approved home health care
4. Hospice care for the terminally ill

All of the following conditions must be met before Medicare Part A benefits can help pay for inpatient hospital care:

1. A doctor prescribes the inpatient hospital care for treatment
2. The care received by the recipient can be provided only in a hospital

3. The hospital is a Medicare participant
4. Neither the hospital's Utilization Review Committee (URC) nor the state's Peer Review Organization (PRO) disapproves the stay

Medicare Part A coverage pays according to benefit periods. A benefit period begins when you enter the hospital and ends when you have been out of a hospital (or, in some cases, a skilled nursing facility) for 60 consecutive days. In the days following the first 60 days, you are responsible for increasing amounts of the cost. (See table below.)

Number of Days	You Pay	Medicare Pays
1–60	the deductible	all costs beyond the deductible
61–90	the daily co-insurance charge	everything beyond a daily co-insurance charge
91–150	the increased daily co-insurance charge	everything beyond an increased daily co-insurance charge

If your hospital stays are separated by more than 60 consecutive days, you will have to pay an additional deductible. Also, Medicare will only cover the first 90 days of your health care needs. The 60 days beyond the first 90 days are called *lifetime reserve days*. These are days that Medicare will pay above $358/day, but you cannot renew these days. Once you have used a lifetime reserve day, you must subtract it from your total number of 60 days. Unlike the other periods of Medicare coverage, lifetime reserve days do not start over if you recover from one illness and do not need health care again for more than 60 days.

One thing Medicare never pays for is the first three pints of whole blood. This cost is called the three-pint deductible.

Medicare Part A Claims—Procedures

Medicare's current system for paying hospitals is the *prospective payment system (PPS)*. Medicare pays the hospital a fixed amount based on the primary diagnosis for each hospital stay. Therefore, the hospital knows in advance the amount it will receive.

Medicare classifies your illness or injury according to one of 490 categories called *diagnosis related groups (DRGs)*. The program assigns each DRG an expected length of stay that serves as a guideline. The drawback of this system is that the hospital has an incentive to discharge you as quickly as possible because it receives the same amount of money no matter what length of time you remain hospitalized. Remember, however, that the hospital should not discharge you until your condition no longer requires inpatient hospital care. If you believe you are being discharged too early, contact your state peer review organization.

Skilled Nursing Facility Benefit

Medicare covers less than 2 percent of all nursing home stays. Its designers never intended the program to cover typical "rest home" situations. The program does cover short rehabilitative stays during which you are receiving intensive therapies performed by professionals for the purpose of improving your condition. Performed in skilled nursing facilities, this is the only type of nursing home care covered by Medicare. Not all nursing homes qualify as skilled nursing facilities.

Number of Days	You Pay	Medicare Pays
1–20	nothing	all
21–100	$89.50/day co-insurance	all charges above $89.50/day
101+	all	nothing

The criteria for skilled nursing facilities coverage is quite specific. You must have spent three days (not including the day of discharge) in a hospital and have been transferred to a Medicare-certified skilled nursing facility (SNF). Once these requirements have been met, the SNF services must be:

1. Skilled care
2. Provided on a daily basis
3. Able to be provided as a practical matter only in an SNF on an inpatient basis
4. As extended treatment for a condition that was treated while you were in the hospital

The providing facility must submit all SNF claims. If it does not do so, you will have no right to appeal should Medicare deny your claim. You have the right to demand that a claim be submitted to Medicare. If your SNF is reluctant to send the claim because the staff believes Medicare will deny it, insist that they send a *no-payment* billing. In this way, the providing SNF is protected and you still have the right to appeal a denial of your claim. (The appeals process will be explained later in this chapter.)

If you are a Medicare beneficiary or Medicaid recipient, be wary of an SNF that asks you for a hefty deposit as a condition of admission. This is in violation of federal law. SNFs cannot ask for deposits or charge for extended care services that are covered by Medicare Part A or Part B. They *can* require a deposit for convenience items such as rental TV sets, but that's about it. If you think an SNF is charging for Medicare-covered services, talk to your Medicare carrier or your local long-term care ombudsman. The ombudsman's number is supposed to be posted in a conspicuous place in each SNF. (To contact or find your local ombudsman, contact the Department of Health and Human Services, Office of Inspector General's toll-free hotline at 1-800-368-5779, or write to OIG Hotline, P.O. Box 17303, Baltimore, MD 21203-7303.)

Home Health Care Benefits

Because of the increasing trend toward less institutionalized care as well as earlier hospital discharges, home health care is more important than ever. Medicare is far from able to provide comprehensive service. In order for you to qualify for home health care benefits, the home health agency must be Medicare-certified and must file a written request for payment. A physician must prescribe the care, which must follow a specific plan. Finally, you must be confined to your home and require skilled care.

Once you meet all of these criteria, Medicare will cover these areas of your home health care:

1. Part-time care provided by, or under the supervision of, a registered nurse
2. Professional physical, occupational, or speech therapy
3. Medical social services provided by a qualified social worker
4. Part-time services of a home health aide as a part of a total plan of care that includes skilled services
5. Medical supplies

Medicare does not cover:

1. Home health services that are not in addition to skilled services
2. Self-administered drugs and biologicals

3. Home-delivered meals
4. Housekeeping services
5. Transportation

The claims procedure for home health care is similar to that of the procedure for skilled nursing facilities. If the agency is reluctant to submit a claim for you because they think Medicare will not cover it, ask them to submit a *no-payment* billing so that you will not lose your right to appeal.

Hospice Care

Medicare pays for most of the care costs for terminally ill patients. This type of care, called *hospice care,* does not attempt to cure patients; rather, it simply attempts to help the terminally ill carry on their lives as normally as possible. During periods of hospice care, Medicare pays for all services in full. The periods are limited to two 90-day periods and one 30-day period for a total of 210 days. A physician or hospice director can ask to extend these periods.

With Medicare hospice coverage, the only financial obligations patients have is 5 percent or $5 (whichever is less) of the cost of outpatient prescriptions, as well as 5 percent (up to $628) of the cost of respite care (i.e., inpatient care aimed at giving family and other unpaid caregivers a break from caring for the terminally ill patient).

For a patient to qualify for Medicare Part A coverage of hospice care, a doctor must certify that the individual is terminally ill. Finally, a Medicare-certified hospice program must provide the care.

The provider of the care must be the one to submit claims for hospice care.

Medicare Part B—The Doctor's Part

Medicare's designers intended Medicare Part B to take up where Medicare Part A leaves off. In general, Medicare Part B coverage extends to medically necessary doctors' services, therapies, outpatient services, medical equipment, and home health care visits.

The following is a more detailed list of the services and supplies covered by Medicare Part B:

1. Physician services (not including Christian Science practitioners or naturopaths)
2. Second opinions regarding elective surgery
3. Optometric services relating to the treatment of cataracts
4. Dentists' services related to surgery of the jaw
5. Chiropractic services relating to treating misalignment of the spine (an X ray taken by an M.D. must demonstrate that a misalignment exists)
6. Services and supplies, including drugs and biologicals that cannot be self-administered
7. Diagnostic X rays, laboratory tests, and other tests
8. X ray, radium, and radioactive isotope therapy, materials, and services
9. Surgical dressings
10. Prosthetic devices that replace all or part of an internal body organ
11. Leg, arm, and neck braces, artificial limbs and eyes

12. Physical and occupational therapy services
13. Outpatient speech pathology
14. Outpatient diagnostic services
15. Dialysis equipment services and supplies
16. Ambulance service
17. Comprehensive outpatient rehabilitation facility services
18. Rural health clinic services
19. Durable medical equipment
20. Home health services if you do not have Medicare Part A coverage
21. Mammography screenings, Pap smears
22. Qualified health care from clinical psychologists, social workers, physician assistants, certified nurse-midwives, registered nurses, anesthetists, or nurse-practitioners

If you are a beneficiary of Medicare Part B, these are the four types of charges for which you are responsible:

1. **Premium**—The monthly premium (in 1995 the monthly premium was $46.10), and the Social Security department automatically deducts this amount from your Social Security check. If you do not receive a Social Security check, the department bills you quarterly.
2. **Deductible**—The Medicare Part B deductible consists of the first $100 (in 1995) of Medicare-approved charges. You have to pay this deductible just once a year. In addition, you must pay for the first three units of whole blood that you require.
3. **Co-insurance**—Beyond the deductible, you will be responsible for 20 percent of the costs.

4. **Excess Charges**—You may also be responsible for the difference between Medicare's approved charge and the actual amount that your provider charges. This difference is called the *excess charge.* A provider's excess charge may not be more than 25 percent of the approved charge or, for office calls, 40 percent of the approved charge.

A major difference between Medicare Part A and Medicare Part B is that for Part B, Medicare will *assign benefits* to the doctor or supplier of medical services. In other words, the person who accepts the assignment submits the claim, and Medicare pays him or her directly. You do not receive any payment, nor do you submit a bill to Medicare. The benefit of this billing method is that the excess charge is eliminated because the provider must accept Medicare's approved amount. Therefore, you will be liable only for the $100 deductible and the 20 percent co-insurance payment.

Not all doctors have to accept assignment unless they are *Medicare participating doctors or suppliers.* These providers are listed in the *Medicare Participating Physician/Supplier Directory,* and they must accept assignment on all Medicare claims for all Medicare patients. You can obtain this free directory from Medicare carriers or from your local Social Security office.

Medicare Part B Claims

The carrier receives all claims within a given state and determines the amount that Medicare will pay. Providers have a year to submit the claim; however, you may submit your own claim if the provider does not do it quickly enough. When you submit your own claim, use Form HCFA-1490S (available at your local Social Security office) and send it to the carrier.

Along with the completed form, you must include an itemized bill showing the following information:

1. Date you received the service
2. Place you received the service
3. Description of the service
4. Charges
5. Name of service provider
6. Your name and health insurance claim number

Included with the payment will be an explanation of a Medicare benefits form called an *Explanation of Medicare Benefits (EOMB),* which explains what Medicare has approved and how much of the bill it will pay.

What Won't Medicare Part A or Medicare Part B Cover?

Medicare never covers the following items:

1. Prevention-oriented services
2. Items covered by a government agency such as the Department of Veterans Affairs
3. Health care received outside of the United States (unless it is emergency care in the nearest Mexican or Canadian hospital, or care received while you were traveling in Canada)
4. Care required as a result of war

5. Convenience items
6. Routine checkups other than Pap smears and mammography screenings
7. Eye exams other than those pertaining to cataract surgery
8. Hearing aids and exams
9. Immunizations except those relating directly to an injury
10. Routine foot care
11. Cosmetic surgery
12. Dental services except for jaw surgery or other den tal services requiring hospitalization
13. Custodial care
14. Charges from Medicare recipients, relatives, or household members
15. Home-delivered meals
16. Domestic services unrelated to the patient's health care
17. Transportation services other than ambulance
18. Items for which automobile, liability, or no-fault insurance will pay
19. Items for which employer group health insurance will pay

How to Appeal a Medicare Denial

Remember, if you feel that Medicare denied your claim unjustly, Congress has stipulated that you have the right to appeal. The appeals procedure is actually quite easy, and you do not need a lawyer. About 70 percent of all Medicare appeals are successful.

Medicare Part A Appeals

If you are appealing a denial of Medicare Part A coverage, there are four steps of which you need to be aware: reconsideration, administrative hearing, Social Security Appeals Council review, and Court of Appeals.

I. Reconsideration. Must be filed no later than 60 days after receipt of written denial from the intermediary. You will submit form HCFA-2649 to your local Social Security Office or intermediary. A written reconsideration performed by the intermediary or peer review organization (PRO) will be issued and mailed to you.

II. Administrative Hearing. Must be filed no later than 60 days after receipt of reconsideration decision denying your claim. The amount in controversy must be a minimum of $100 ($200 for PRO decisions). You will submit form HA-501-U5 to your local Social Security office. An Administrative Law Judge (ALJ) will set up a hearing during which the ALJ will listen to all testimony and examine all relevant evidence. This hearing is not adversarial or formal, so it is not necessary for a lawyer to be present to represent you.

III. Social Security Appeals Council Review. Must be filed no later than 60 days after receipt of administrative hearing decision. The amount in controversy must be a minimum of $100. You will submit form HA-520-U5 to the Social Security Appeals Council. This level of appeal is held "on the record" and you will not be allowed to appear in person. This type of appeal rarely results in a decision favorable to the beneficiary and should be pursued only if the beneficiary is prepared to go to the U.S. District Court.

IV. U.S. District Court of Appeal. Must be filed no later than 60 days after receipt of Appeals Council decision. The amount in controversy must be a minimum of $1,000. If you reach this point in the appeals process, you should consult an attorney.

Medicare Part B Appeals

If you are appealing a Medicare Part B denial, there are three steps you need to know about: review, hearing, and U.S. District Court review:

I. Review. Must be filed no later than six months after receipt of an EOMB. You will submit form HCFA-1964 to your local Social Security office or your Medicare Part B carrier. Many of these appeals involve "approved charge" controversies.

II. Hearing. Must be filed no later than six months after receipt of review decision, and the amount in controversy must be a minimum of $100. You will submit form HCFA-1965 to your local Social Security office. You may represent yourself at this hearing, which an ALJ sets up. The hearing is informal.

III. U.S. District Court. At this point, if you are appealing a Medicare Part B denial, it is best to consult a lawyer because the next step will, in all likelihood, be a formal appeal in a United States District Court.

WHEN MEDICARE ISN'T ENOUGH

From everything we've said thus far, it should be apparent that Medicare alone will not cover all of your health care costs. Even after you have unraveled the twists and turns of Medicare and you are receiving the maximum compensation, you probably will not be able to afford to pay for the kind of care you may need or want. What should you do? You can investigate private health insurance, a confusing, complex business. Nonetheless, it is essential that you attempt to understand it.

There are four main areas of health care that Medicare does not cover:

I. Hospital Costs. In 1995, a hospital stay might require you to pay a $716 deductible, $179 per day for days 61–90, $358 per day for any reserve days used, all costs after your reserve days are completed, and $89.50 per day for days 21–100 of skilled nursing care.

II. Doctor Bills. If the physician does not accept Medicare reimbursement as full payment, you pay a $100 deductible, 20 percent of all Medicare-approved costs, all excess charges, and all routine exams as well as all eye and dental care costs.

III. Prescription Drugs. Unless you are hospitalized or in a skilled nursing facility, you are responsible for all costs.

IV. Nursing Home Care. Medicare does not cover such care unless the standards for receiving benefits in a skilled nursing facility are met. According to the Health Insurance

Association of America, the average cost of a year in a nursing home is $36,000. The average cost of a year of home health care is $12,000. (Medicare covers medical and rehabilitation services, but long-term care is an out-of-pocket expense for most people.) The *Journal of Taxation of Estates and Trusts* says that your chances of using some form of long-term care over the age of 65 are nearly 50 percent. Considering these statistics, and the fact that Medicare covers only 2 percent of nursing home costs, long-term care insurance may give you the added security you need.

Although planning for nursing home care is not something most people want to think about, the sooner you start, the more money you're apt to save. If you're 50 years old, a policy covering $80 a day in nursing home benefits, with a 20-day deductible period, costs around $480 a year. At age 65 the same policy costs about $1,100 a year and close to $4,000 as you reach 80. Policies are available through the American Association of Retired Persons, some employers, and private insurers.

For more information on long-term care insurance, contact:

THE AMERICAN COUNCIL OF LIFE INSURANCE/
    HEALTH INSURANCE ASSOCIATION OF AMERICA
1001 Pennsylvania Ave. NW
Washington, DC 20004
202-624-2000

Seven Tips on Selecting a Nursing Home

1. Check that the interior and grounds of the home are clean and well maintained.

2. Observe and talk with the residents. See if they appear clean, comfortable, and appropriately dressed.
3. Try to see if there is adequate staff, and observe how caring they are.
4. Make sure a doctor is available for emergencies.
5. Make sure the home doesn't have a bad odor.
6. Check that the bedrooms open onto a corridor and have windows, as required by law.
7. Ask whether there's a resident council program that meets regularly and allows residents to recommend changes.

For more information regarding nursing homes, contact:

> THE AMERICAN HEALTH CARE ASSOCIATION
> 1201 L St. NW
> Washington, DC 20005
> 202-842-4444

Ask for brochures entitled: *Thinking About a Nursing Home, Physician Services in the Long-term Care Facility, Here's Help: Myths and Realities of Living in a Nursing Home,* and *Here's Help: Special Programs Within Nursing Homes.*

Assisted Living Facilities

Assisted living facilities allow people to live on their own, but in a safer setting than their own house or apartment. Residents are offered help with meals, shopping, and housekeeping, as well as bathing and taking medications. Unlike nursing homes, these institutions are not federally regulated. Before choosing one, ask the same questions you would ask about a nursing home.

The costs vary from $900 a month to more than $3,000 a month. Medicare will not cover these costs. A few long-term care insurance policies cover assisted living expenses as an "alternative care benefit," but such policies are relatively new.

Hospice Care

Hospices are designed to allow terminally ill people to die with dignity, providing for their physical as well as emotional and spiritual needs. In the United States, 90 percent of hospice services are given to patients at home, and 10 percent are given in nursing homes or hospice centers. Patients go into the hospice facility only when their disease requires more round-the-clock monitoring, or when their families need a break.

If you're covered under Medicare and accepted by a Medicare-approved hospice, almost the entire cost of your care will be covered. Most private health insurance policies and many employer policies also pay for hospice care.

For more information contact the following resources:

NATIONAL HOSPICE ORGANIZATION
1901 N. Moore St., Suite 901
Arlington, VA 22209
1-800-658-8898

AMERICAN ASSOCIATION OF HOMES AND SERVICES
  FOR THE AGING
Communications Office
901 E St. NW, Suite 500
Washington, DC 20004-2037
202-783-2242

Filling Medicare's Gaps

If you look at the various options carefully and buy selectively, you will be able to fill most but not all (it is next to impossible to purchase total coverage) of the gaps in Medicare coverage without falling into the trap of paying more than necessary for coverage you already have. (Many Americans unwittingly pay for duplicate coverage.)

Private health insurance is supplemental health insurance, and it will usually not pay for a service that Medicare has already rejected.

There are five basic options in supplemental health insurance: indemnity plans, limited policies, employer plans, health maintenance organizations, and Medicare supplements.

I. Indemnity Plans. This policy is very simple. It pays a fixed dollar amount directly to you per day, week, or month while you are in the hospital.

II. Limited Policies. There are three kinds of limited coverage policies: *Long-term care policies* usually pay an indemnity for each day that you require nursing home care. *Specific disease policies* pay an indemnity per day of hospitalization for a certain disease or injury. *Medical-surgical policies* pay a specific amount toward covered medical or surgical expenses and could pay for some charges above the Medicare-approved charges. However, such policies often duplicate coverage already provided by Medicare.

III. Employer Continuation and Conversion Plans. This type of coverage is a portion of your retirement benefits. This policy may pay above the Medicare-approved charge. Check with your employer to find out exactly what will be covered.

IV. Health Maintenance Organizations. This type of coverage, often called HMOs, works in such a way that your provider is also your insurance company. You pay a monthly premium only; however, you are limited to seeking health care from a specific group of providers who are members of your HMO. Your primary care physician serves as the gatekeeper; you need his or her referral in order to see a specialist or doctor outside of the plan. According to the July/August issue of *New Choices for Retirement Living,* your primary care physician has reason to limit your referrals to specialists. Your physician's financial compensation and future participation in the HMO is partly determined by restricting outside referrals. If you often need medical care beyond the scope of your primary physician, find out whether a plan covers a broad range of specialized care before you buy it. Despite the restrictions of HMOs, they are probably the most comprehensive way to fill in Medicare's gaps.

For more information on HMOs, write to:

THE AMERICAN COUNCIL ON SCIENCE AND HEALTH
1995 Broadway, 16th Floor
New York, NY 10023-5860

Or call the American Association of Retired Persons at 1-800-424-3410 and ask for the FREE brochure, *Managed Care.*

V. Medicare Supplements or Medigap Plans. This type of policy often covers cost gaps like deductibles and co-insurance. However, these plans rarely pay for charges that Medicare does not cover, such as long-term care.

All Medigap policies are lettered A through J. Your coverage and premiums increase as you go down the alphabet. For example, plans A through J all cover basic benefits such as co-insurance and lifetime reserve days (91–150). But additional benefits, such as deductible, prescription drugs, and at-home recovery, vary according to plan. Don't feel compelled to buy the most extensive or expensive plan. For example, plan C is among the most popular, but it doesn't provide much more coverage than plan B, which costs less.

When you are on Medicare and have a Medigap policy, you do not need additional types of coverage

Until 1992, insurance companies were allowed to sell medical insurance that supplemented Medicare even if it included areas of coverage you already had. Now insurers have to disclose how a policy overlaps Medicare, but they don't have to disclose how it overlaps the other Medigap policies. Remember, you need only one Medigap policy. For example, nine of the ten Medigap policies pay Medicare's hospital deductible. Buying an additional Medigap plan would most likely duplicate this coverage, which means you'd be paying more for the same thing.

For free information and help regarding Medigap issues, contact your local agency on aging or state insurance department. Every state offers a free insurance counseling program. Counselors can help you avoid costly duplication between policies and determine whether you have any important needs your policies aren't covering. Local senior centers also provide guidance; call the U.S. Administration on Aging's ElderCare Locator Hotline at 1-800-677-1116 for local resources.

Perhaps the best advice you will receive regarding supplemental health insurance is that your goal should be to find the most comprehensive policy that will best fill in the gaps of your Medicare coverage. It is very important to obtain as much information as possible about many policies. Do not buy the first one you investigate.

Six Tips on Shopping for Health Insurance

1. Ask for an outline of coverage that will explain the basics of the policy.
2. Answer all health questions on the application honestly.
3. Read everything before you sign anything.
4. If you don't understand something, ASK.
5. Verify with your state's insurance department that the company you are considering is licensed.
6. Do not buy under pressure.

For more information about Medicare, consult the following resources:

Mastering the Medicare Maze
CENTER FOR PUBLIC REPRESENTATION, INC.
121 S. Pinckney St.
Madison, WI 53703

The Medicare Handbook
U.S. DEPARTMENT OF HEALTH AND HUMAN SERVICES
Health Care Financing Administration
6325 Security Blvd.
Baltimore, MD 21207

Medicare Hotline, 1-800-638-6833

MEDICARE PART A
INTERMEDIARIES LIST

Some home health agencies may choose alternative intermediaries. In addition, some home health agency chains
that serve more than one region may choose to be serviced
by only one of their regional intermediaries. Check with
your local home health agency to be sure of its intermediary.

**Connecticut, Maine,
Massachusetts, New
Hampshire, Rhode Island,
and Vermont:**

ASSOCIATED HOSPITAL SERVICE
OF MAINE
110 Free St.
Portland, ME 04101
(207) 822-7000

**Delaware, District of
Columbia, Maryland,
Pennsylvania, Virginia,
and West Virginia:**

BLUE CROSS OF GREATER
PENNSYLVANIA
1901 Market St.
Philadelphia, PA 19103
(215) 241-2400

Kentucky, North Carolina, South Carolina, and Tennessee:

BLUE CROSS AND BLUE SHIELD
OF SOUTH CAROLINA
Fontaine Business Center
300 Arbor Lake Dr.
Suite 1300
Columbia, SC 29223
(803) 788-3860

Alabama, Florida, Georgia, and Mississippi:

MEDICARE ADMINISTRATION
25400 U.S. Hwy. 19N, Suite 135
Clearwater, FL 34623-2193
(813) 796-8292

Wisconsin, Michigan, New Jersey, New York, Puerto Rico, Minnesota, and the U.S. Virgin Islands:

BLUE CROSS AND BLUE SHIELD
UNITED OF WISCONSIN
P.O. Box 2025
Milwaukee, WI 53202
(414) 226-5000

Illinois, Indiana, and Ohio:

HEALTH CARE SERVICES
CORPORATION
233 N. Michigan Ave.
Chicago, IL 60601
(312) 938-6262

Alaska, Arizona, California, Hawaii, Idaho, Oregon, Nevada, and Washington:

BLUE CROSS OF CALIFORNIA
2155 Oxnard St.
Woodland Hills, CA 91367
(818) 703-2345

Arkansas, Louisiana, New Mexico, Oklahoma, and Texas:

NEW MEXICO BLUE CROSS AND
BLUE SHIELD, INC.
12800 Indian School Rd. NE
P.O. Box 11566
Albuquerque, NM 87192
(505) 291-3500

Colorado, Iowa, Kansas, Missouri, Montana, Nebraska, North Dakota, South Dakota, Utah, and Wyoming:

BLUE CROSS OF IOWA, INC.
636 Grand Ave.
Station 28
Des Moines, IA 50309
(515) 245-4500

HOSPICES

BLUE CROSS/BLUE SHIELD UNITED OF WISCONSIN
Will service all states east of the Mississippi River (see address under General Intermediaries).

BLUE CROSS OF CALIFORNIA
Will service all states west of the Mississippi River (Minnesota and Louisianaare included in this service area) (see address under General Intermediaries).

GENERAL INTERMEDIARIES

NOTE: Many intermediaries who are not connected with Blue Cross do not serve a particular region. These intermediaries will be listed after the state listing under the heading "Commercial Independent Intermediaries." To be absolutely sure of your provider's intermediary, ask your provider.

Alabama
BLUE CROSS AND BLUE SHIELD
    OF ALABAMA
450 Riverchase Pkwy. E.
Birmingham, AL 35298
(205) 988-2100

Alaska
    See BLUE CROSS OF
WASHINGTON/ALASKA

Arizona
BLUE CROSS AND BLUE SHIELD
    OF ARIZONA, INC.
P.O. Box 37700
Phoenix, AZ 85069
(602) 864-4400
1-800-232-2345

Arkansas
ARKANSAS BLUE CROSS AND
    BLUE SHIELD, INC.
601 Gaines St.
Little Rock, AR 72201
(501) 378-2000

California
BLUE CROSS OF CALIFORNIA
2155 Oxnard St.
Woodland Hills, CA 91367
(818) 703-2345

Colorado
BLUE CROSS/BLUE SHIELD
    OF COLORADO
700 Broadway
Denver, CO 80273
(303) 844-6149

Connecticut

BLUE CROSS AND BLUE SHIELD
OF CONNECTICUT, INC.
370 Bassett Rd.
North Haven, CT 06473
(203) 239-4911

Delaware

BLUE CROSS AND BLUE SHIELD
OF DELAWARE, INC.
One Brandywine Gateway
P.O. Box 8770
Wilmington, DE 19899
(302) 421-3000

District of Columbia

See BLUE CROSS OF MARYLAND

Florida

BLUE CROSS AND BLUE SHIELD
OF FLORIDA, INC.
P.O. Box 2711
Jacksonville, FL 32231
(904) 791-6111

Georgia

BLUE CROSS OF GEORGIA, INC.
2357 Warm Springs Rd.
P.O. Box 7368
Columbus, GA 31908
(706) 571-5371

Hawaii

HAWAII MEDICAL SERVICE
ASSOCIATION
818 Keeaumoku
P.O. Box 860
Honolulu, HI 96808
(808) 944-2324

Idaho

See BLUE CROSS OF OREGON

Illinois

HEALTH CARE SERVICE CORP.
233 North Michigan Ave.
Chicago, IL 60601
(312) 938-6206

Indiana

ASSOCIATED INSURANCE COMPANIES,
INC.
8320 Craig St., Suite 100
Indianapolis, IN 46250-0452
(317) 841-4400

Iowa

BLUE CROSS OF IOWA
636 Grand Ave.
Station 28
Des Moines, IA 50307
(515) 245-4500

Kansas

BLUE CROSS KANSAS, INC.
1133 Topeka Blvd.
P.O. Box 239
Topeka, KS 66601
(913) 232-1000

Kentucky

BLUE CROSS AND BLUE SHIELD
OF KENTUCKY, INC.
9901 Linn Station Rd.
Louisville, KY 40223
(502) 423-2011

Louisiana

See BLUE CROSS OF MISSISSIPPI

Maine

Associated Hospital Service
   of Maine
110 Free St.
Portland, ME 04101
(207) 822-7000

Maryland

Maryland Blue Shield, Inc.
1946 Green Spring Dr.
Timonium, MD 21093
(410) 581-3000

Massachusetts

Blue Cross of Massachusetts
100 Summer St.
Boston, MA 02106
(617) 956-2532

Michigan

Blue Cross and Blue Shield
   of Michigan
600 Lafayette East
Detroit, MI 48226
(313) 225-8200

Minnesota

Blue Cross and Blue Shield
   of Minnesota
3535 Blue Cross Rd.
St. Paul, MN 55164
(612) 456-8000

Mississippi

Blue Cross and Blue Shield
   of Mississippi
P.O. Box 23035
Jackson, MS 39225
(601) 932-3704

Missouri

Blue Cross and Blue Shield
   of Missouri
4444 Forest Park
St. Louis, MO 63108
(314) 658-4351
1-800-392-8740

Montana

Blue Cross and Blue Shield
   of Montana
3360 10th Ave. S.
Great Falls, MT 59601
(406) 791-4000

Nebraska

Blue Cross and Blue Shield
   of Nebraska
P.O. Box 24563
West Omaha Station
Omaha, NE 68124
(402) 390-1850

Nevada

   See Blue Cross of Arizona

New Hampshire

Blue Cross/Blue Shield
   of New Hampshire-Vermont
Two Pillsbury St.
Concord, NH 03301
(603) 224-9511

New Jersey

Blue Cross and Blue Shield
   of New Jersey
33 Washington St.
Newark, NJ 07102
(201) 456-2000

New Mexico

NEW MEXICO BLUE CROSS AND
  BLUE SHIELD, INC.
12800 Indian School Rd. NE
 P.O. Box 13597
Albuquerque, NM 87112-3597
(505) 291-3500

New York

NEW YORK BLUE CROSS MEDICARE
  PART A CLAIMS PROCESSING
P.O. Box 4846
Syracuse, NY 13221
(315) 474-4121

North Carolina

BLUE CROSS AND BLUE SHIELD
  OF NORTH CAROLINA
P.O. Box 2291
Durham, NC 27702
(919) 688-5528

North Dakota

BLUE CROSS/BLUE SHIELD
  OF NORTH DAKOTA
4510 13th Ave. SW
Fargo, ND 58121
(701) 282-1100

Ohio

COMMUNITY MUTUAL INSURANCE
  COMPANY
Atrium Two, Suite 2600
221 E. 4th St.
Cincinnati, OH 45202
(513) 872-8100

Oklahoma

OKLAHOMA BLUE CROSS/
  BLUE SHIELD
1215 S. Boulder Ave.
Tulsa, OK 74119
(918) 560-2090

Oregon

BLUE CROSS AND BLUE SHIELD
  OF OREGON
P.O. Box 8110
Portland, OR 97207
(503) 721-7007

Pennsylvania

INDEPENDENCE BLUE CROSS
1901 Market St.
Philadelphia, PA 19103
(215) 241-2400

BLUE CROSS OF WESTERN
  PENNSYLVANIA
5th Avenue Pl.
Suite 1114
Pittsburgh, PA 15222
(412) 255-7000
1-800-537-3426

AETNA LIFE AND CASUALTY
501 Office Center Dr.
Fort Washington, PA 19034
(215) 643-7200

Puerto Rico

COOPERATIVE DE SEGUROS
  DE VIDA DE PUERTO RICO
GPO Box 3428
San Juan, PR 00936-3428
(809) 758-9720

Rhode Island
BLUE CROSS OF RHODE ISLAND
444 Westminster Mall
Providence, RI 02901
(401) 272-8500

South Carolina
BLUE CROSS AND BLUE SHIELD
OF SOUTH CAROLINA
Fontaine Business Center
300 Arbor Lake Dr.
Suite 1300
Columbia, SC 29223
(803) 788-3860

South Dakota
see BLUE CROSS OF IOWA

Tennessee
BLUE CROSS AND BLUE SHIELD
OF TENNESSEE
801 Pine St.
Chattanooga, TN 37402
(615) 755-5779

Texas
BLUE CROSS AND BLUE SHIELD
OF TEXAS, INC.
901 S. Central Expwy.
P.O. Box 833815
Richardson, TX 75083-3815
(214) 766-6900

Utah
BLUE CROSS AND BLUE SHIELD
OF UTAH
2455 Parley's Way
P.O. Box 30270
Salt Lake City, UT 84130
(801) 487-6447
1-800-824-2716

Vermont
See BLUE CROSS OF
NEW HAMPSHIRE

Virgin Islands
See BLUE CROSS OF
PUERTO RICO

Virginia
BLUE CROSS OF VIRGINIA
602 Jefferson St. SE
P.O. Box 12201
Roanoke, VA 24023-2201
(703) 985-5000

Washington
BLUE CROSS OF
WASHINGTON/ALASKA
7001-220th SW
P.O. Box 2847
Mountlake Terrace, WA 98043
(206) 670-4000

West Virginia
See BLUE CROSS OF VIRGINIA

Wisconsin
BLUE CROSS AND BLUE SHIELD
UNITED OF WISCONSIN
P.O. Box 2025
Milwaukee, WI 53201
(414) 226-5000

Wyoming
BLUE CROSS AND BLUE SHIELD
OF WYOMING
4000 House Ave.
P.O. Box 108
Cheyenne, WY 82003
(307) 634-1393

COMMERCIAL INDEPENDENT INTERMEDIARIES

AETNA LIFE AND CASUALTY COMPANY (HOME OFFICE)
Medicare Administration-M323
151 Farmington Ave.
Hartford, CT 06156
(203) 273-0123

FIELD OFFICES—PART A AUDIT/REIMBURSEMENT

AETNA LIFE AND
 CASUALTY-MEDICARE
25400 U.S. Highway 19N
Suite 135
Clearwater, FL 34623-2193
(813) 796-8292

AETNA LIFE AND CASUALTY
 COMPANY-MEDICARE
4507 North Sterling Ave.
4th Floor
Peoria, IL 61615
(309) 686-2300

AETNA LIFE AND CASUALTY
 MEDICARE CLAIMS DIVISION
4600 Kietzke Ln.
Unit 134D
Reno, NV 89502
(702) 825-2300

AETNA LIFE AND CASUALTY
 COMPANY-MEDICARE
Fort Washington
P.O. Drawer 548
Fort Washington, PA 19034
(215) 643-7200

AETNA LIFE AND
 CASUALTY MEDICARE
1353 Redwood Way
Petaluma, CA 94954
(707) 664-0365

COOPERATIVE DE
 SEGUROS DE VIDA DE
 PUERTO RICO
GPO Box 3428
San Juan, PR 00936-3428
(809) 764-9069

HAWAII MEDICAL SERVICE
 ASSOCIATION
818 Keeaumoku
P.O. Box 860
Honolulu, HI 96808
(808) 944-2324

MUTUAL OF OMAHA INSURANCE
 COMPANY
P.O. Box 1602
Omaha, NE 68101
(402) 978-2860

THE TRAVELERS INSURANCE COMPANY

FIELD OFFICES—PART A AUDIT/REIMBURSEMENT

THE TRAVELERS INSURANCE
COMPANY
P.O. Box 2002
New Haven, CT 06536
(203) 281-2000

MEDICARE PART A
90 Merrick Ave.
P.O. Box 7004
East Meadows, NY 11554
(516) 296-2000

MEDICARE AUDIT
14000 Travelers Tower
26555 Evergreen Rd.
Southfield, MI 48706
(313) 423-2308

MEDICARE PART B
CARRIERS LIST

Alabama
MEDICARE BLUE CROSS-
  BLUE SHIELD OF ALABAMA
P.O. Box C-140
Birmingham, AL 35283
(205) 988-2100
1-800-292-8855

Alaska
MEDICARE AETNA LIFE
  AND CASUALTY
200 SW Market
P.O. Box 1998
Portland, OR 97207-1998
(503) 222-6831
1-800-547-6333

American Samoa
  See HAWAII

Arizona
MEDICARE AETNA LIFE
  AND CASUALTY
10000 N. 31st Ave.
P.O. Box 37200
Phoenix, AZ 85069
(602) 870-6203
1-800-352-0411

Arkansas
MEDICARE ARKANSAS BLUE CROSS
  AND BLUE SHIELD
P.O. Box 1418
Little Rock, AR 72203
(501) 378-2000
1-800-482-5525

California
**Counties of: Los Angeles, Orange,
San Diego, Ventura, Imperial,
San Luis Obispo, Santa Barbara**
MEDICARE TRANSAMERICA
  OCCIDENTAL LIFE INSURANCE CO.
Box 54905
Terminal Annex
Los Angeles, CA 90054-0905
(213) 748-2311
1-800-252-9020

Rest of State:
BLUE SHIELD OF CALIFORNIA
P.O. Box 7013
San Francisco, CA 94120
(916) 743-1583
(714) 824-0900
1-800-952-8627

Colorado

MEDICARE-BLUE CROSS/
  BLUE SHIELD OF COLORADO
700 Broadway
Denver, CO 80273
(303) 831-2661
1-800-332-6681

Connecticut

THE TRAVELERS INSURANCE
  COMPANY
538 Preston Ave.
P.O. Box 9000
Meriden, CT 06454-9000
(203) 728-6783
1-800-982-6819

Delaware

MEDICARE PENNSYLVANIA
  BLUE SHIELD
P.O. Box 890200
Camp Hill, PA 17089-0200
(717) 763- 3151
1-800-851-3535

Florida

BLUE CROSS AND BLUE SHIELD
  OF FLORIDA, INC.
P.O. Box 2360
Jacksonville, FL 32231
(904) 791-6111
1-800-333-7586

Georgia

AETNA LIFE AND CASUALTY
P.O. Box 60010
Savannah, GA 31402-0010
(912) 921-3010
1-800-727-0827

Hawaii

MEDICARE AETNA LIFE
  AND CASUALTY
P.O. Box 3947
Honolulu, HI 96812-3947
(808) 524-1240
1-800-272-0827

Idaho

MEDICARE EQUICOR, INC.
3140 N. Lakeharbor Ln.
Suite 254
P.O. Box 8084
Boise, ID 83707-2048
(208) 342-7763
1-800-627-2782

Illinois

BLUE CROSS/BLUE SHIELD
  OF ILLINOIS
P.O. Box 4422
Marion, IL 62959
(312) 938-8000
1-800-642-6930

Indiana

MEDICARE PART B
  ASSOCIATED INSURANCE
  COMPANIES
P.O. Box 240
Indianapolis, IN 46206-0240
(317) 842-4151
1-800-622-4792

Iowa

MEDICARE BLUE SHIELD OF IOWA
636 Grand, Station 28
Des Moines, IA 50309
(515) 245-4785
1-800-532-1285

Kansas
Counties of: Johnson, Wyandotte

MEDICARE BLUE SHIELD
OF KANSAS CITY
P.O. Box 169
Kansas City, MO 64141
(816) 561-0900
1-800-892-5900

Rest of State:

MEDICARE BLUE SHIELD
OF KANSAS, INC.
P.O. Box 239
Topeka, KS 66601
(913) 232-3773
1-800-432-3531

Kentucky

MEDICARE PART B
BLUE CROSS AND BLUE SHIELD
OF KENTUCKY
100 E. Vine St., 6th Floor
Lexington, KY 40517
(606) 233-1436
1-800-999-7608

Louisiana

LOUISIANA BLUE CROSS/
BLUE SHIELD
P.O. Box 95024
Baton Rouge, LA 70895-9024
(504) 927-3490
1-800-462-9666

Maine

BLUE SHIELD OF MASSACHUSETTS
TRI-STATE
P.O. Box 1010
Biddeford, ME 04405
(207) 282-5991
1-800-492-0919

Maryland
Counties of: Montgomery,
Prince Georges

MEDICARE PENNSYLVANIA
BLUE SHIELD
P.O. Box 890100
Camp Hill, PA 17089-0100
(717) 763-3151
1-800-233-1124

Rest of State:

MARYLAND BLUE SHIELD, INC.
1946 Green Spring Dr.
Timonium, MD 21093
(410) 581-3000
1-800-492-4795

Massachusetts

MEDICARE BLUE SHIELD
OF MASSACHUSETTS, INC.
1022 Hingham St.
Rockland, MA 02371
(617) 956-2140
1-800-882-1228

Michigan

MEDICARE PART B
  MICHIGAN BLUE CROSS/
  BLUE SHIELD
P.O. Box 2201
Detroit, MI 48231
(313) 225-8200

In Area Code 313:
1-800-482-4045

In Area Code 517:
1-800-322-0607

In Area Code 616:
1-800-442-8020

In Area Code 906:
1-800-562-7802

Minnesota
Counties of: Anoka, Dakota, Filmore, Goodhue, Hennepin, Houston, Olmstead, Ramsey, Wabasha, Washington, Winona
MEDICARE
  THE TRAVELERS INSURANCE CO.
8120 Penn Ave. South
Bloomington, MN 55431
(612) 884-7111
1-800-352-2762

Rest of State:
BLUE CROSS/BLUE SHIELD
  OF MINNESOTA
P.O. Box 64357
St. Paul, MN 55164
(612) 456-5070
1-800-456-5070

Mississippi
MEDICARE
  THE TRAVELERS INSURANCE CO.
P.O. Box 22545
Jackson, MS 39205-2545
(601) 956-0372
1-800-682-5417

Missouri
Counties of: Andrew, Atchison, Bates, Benton, Buchanan, Caldwell, Carroll, Cass, Clay, Clinton, Daviess, DeKalb, Gentry, Grundy, Harrison, Henry, Holt, Jackson, Johnson, Lafayette, Livingston, Mercer, Nodaway, Pettis, Platte, Ray, St. Clair, Saline, Vernon, Worth
MEDICARE BLUE SHIELD
  OF KANSAS CITY
P.O. Box 169
Kansas City, MO 64141
(816) 561-0900
1-800-892-5900

Rest of State:
MEDICARE
  GENERAL AMERICAN LIFE
  INSURANCE COMPANY
P.O. Box 505
St. Louis, MO 63166
(314) 843-8880
1-800-392-3070

Montana
MEDICARE MONTANA PHYSICIANS'
  SERVICE
P.O. Box 4310
Helena, MT 59604
(406) 444-8350
1-800-332-6146

Nebraska
BLUE CROSS/BLUE SHIELD
OF KANSAS
1133 Topeka Blvd.
P.O. Box 3512
Topeka, KS 66601-3512
(913) 232-3773
1-800-633-1113

Nevada
MEDICARE AETNA LIFE AND
CASUALTY
P.O. Box 37230
Phoenix, AZ 85069
(602) 870-6203
1-800-528-0311

New Hampshire
See MAINE
1-800-447-1142

New Jersey
MEDICARE PENNSYLVANIA
BLUE SHIELD
P.O. Box 400010
Harrisburg, PA 17140-0010
(717) 763-3151
1-800-462-9306

New Mexico
AETNA LIFE AND CASUALTY
P.O. Box 25500
Oklahoma City, OK 73125-0500
(505) 843-7771
1-800-423-2925

New York
**Counties of: Bronx, Columbia,
Delaware, Dutchess, Greene,
Kings, Nassau, New York, Orange,
Putnam, Richmond, Rockland,
Suffolk, Sullivan, Ulster,
Westchester**
EMPIRE BLUE CROSS AND
BLUE SHIELD
P.O. Box 100
Yorktown Heights, NY 10598
(212) 490-4444
1-800-442-8430

County of: Queens
MEDICARE GROUP HEALTH, INC.
P.O. Box 1608
Ansonia Station
New York, NY 10023
(212) 721-1770

Rest of State:
MEDICARE BLUE SHIELD
OF WESTERN NEW YORK
P.O. Box 5600
Binghamton, NY 13902-0600
(607) 772-6906
1-800-252-6550

North Carolina
EQUICOR, INC.
P.O. Box 671
Nashville, TN 37202
(919) 665-0380
1-800-672-3071

North Dakota

MEDICARE BLUE SHIELD
OF NORTH DAKOTA
4510 13th Ave. SW
Fargo, ND 58121-0001
(701) 282-1100
1-800-247-2267

Ohio

MEDICARE NATIONWIDE MUTUAL
INSURANCE CO.
P.O. Box 57
Columbus, OH 43216
(614) 249-7157
1-800-282-0530

Oklahoma

MEDICARE AETNA LIFE
AND CASUALTY
701 NW 63rd St., 3rd Floor
Oklahoma City, OK 73116-7693
(405) 848-7711
1-800-522-9079

Oregon

MEDICARE AETNA LIFE
AND CASUALTY
200 SW Market St.
P.O. Box 1997
Portland, OR 97207-1997
(503) 222-6831
1-800-452-0125

Pennsylvania

MEDICARE PENNSYLVANIA
BLUE SHIELD
P.O. Box 890065
Blue Shield Bldg.
Camp Hill, PA 17089-0065
(717) 763-3151
1-800-382-1274

Puerto Rico

MEDICARE SEGUROS DE SERVICIO
DE SALUD DE PUERTO RICO
Call Box 71391
San Juan, PR 00936
(809) 749-4900
1-800-462-7015

Rhode Island

MEDICARE BLUE SHIELD OF
RHODE ISLAND
444 Westminster Mall
Providence, RI 02901
(401) 861-2273
1-800-662-5170

South Carolina

MEDICARE BLUE CROSS AND
BLUE SHIELD OF SOUTH
CAROLINA
Fontaine Rd. Business Ctr.
300 Arbor Lake Dr.
Suite 300
Columbus, SC 29223
(803) 754-1968
1-800-868-252

South Dakota

MEDICARE-BLUE CROSS/
BLUE SHIELD OF NORTH DAKOTA
4510 13th Ave. SW
Fargo, ND 58121-0001
(701) 282-1100
1-800-437-4762

Tennessee

MEDICARE EQUICOR, INC.
P.O. Box 671
Nashville, TN 37202
(615) 244-5600
1-800-342-8900

Texas

MEDICARE BLUE CROSS AND
  BLUE SHIELD OF TEXAS, INC.
P.O. Box 660031
Dallas, TX 75266-0031
(214) 235-3433
1-800-442-2620

Utah

MEDICARE BLUE CROSS AND
  BLUE SHIELD OF UTAH
P.O. Box 30270
2455 Parley's Way
Salt Lake City, UT
84130-0270
(801) 481-6196
1-800-824-2716

Vermont

See MAINE

Virginia

Counties of: Arlington, Fairfax
Cities of: Alexandria, Falls
Church, Fairfax

See PENNSYLVANIA

Rest of State:

MEDICARE
  THE TRAVELERS INSURANCE CO.
P.O. Box 26463
Richmond, VA 23261
(804) 254-4130
1-800-552-3423

U.S. Virgin Islands

See PUERTO RICO

Washington

Mail to your local Medical
Service Bureau. If you do not
know which bureau handles your
claim, mail to:

KING COUNTY MEDICAL
  BLUE SHIELD
P.O. Box 21248
Seattle, WA 98111
(206) 464-3711
1-800-422-4087

West Virginia

See OHIO

Wisconsin

MEDICARE WISCONSIN PHYSICIANS'
  SERVICE
P.O. Box 1787
Madison, WI 53708
(608) 221-3330
1-800-362-7221

Wyoming

BLUE CROSS/BLUE SHIELD
  OF WYOMING
P.O. Box 108
Cheyenne, WY 82003
(307) 632-9381
1-800-442-2371

TRAVEL AND LEISURE

With retirement come opportunities. After years of hard work, you are finally afforded the chance to catch up on the things that you like to do. For many, that includes traveling. Traveling can mean visiting your grandchildren a few hundred miles away to exploring the deepest reaches of a South American rain forest. Whatever your interests are, the following travel information has been collected with you in mind and can help make your next trip a memorable event.

This section is meant as an overview and contains informative tips, valuable offers, and pertinent resources to assist you as you plan an enjoyable as well as money-saving vacation. Wherever possible, phone numbers and addresses have been included, allowing you to pursue a more thorough explanation of the material presented.

TRAVEL TIPS

3 TIPS AND TRAPS FOR SAFE TRIPS

1. To find the lowest airfare, ask your travel agent if it would be cheaper to fly on a different day, a different time of day, during a different week of the month, at an earlier departure date, or at designated off-peak times. Also, ask your travel agent if there are any special seasonal or promotional fares available. Be sure to ask about other airlines. Travel agents may promote particular airlines unless you specifically ask for quotes on others. Before finally agreeing to pay for a flight, ask directly if the agent knows any way you could get a lower fare.

2. Make luggage "tamper evident" by wrapping it with bright electrical or colored tape. Crooked baggage handlers will be less likely to break the seal. And if they do, you'll know immediately and can report the theft before leaving the terminal.

3. If you are not a frequent traveler, notify your bank if you will be using your automated teller machine (ATM) card to make cash withdrawals overseas. A series of withdrawals from unexpected places might lead your bank to block your account. Cardholders should check with their banks to be sure a primary account has been designated (checking or savings).

If your primary account is not designated by your U.S. bank, the overseas bank may decide which account the transaction will affect or, in some cases, may deny the request. Also, many keypads of ATMs outside the United States have numbers, not letters. Before going overseas, know the numeric equivalent of your personal identification number (PIN).

4 ROAD SAFETY HINTS FOR SENIORS

Knowing the problems that arise as we age, and how to compensate for them, can keep you driving safely for years to come. Most people reach age 65 before their driving deteriorates significantly. Nevertheless, the years do begin to take their toll as we get older. Assess your driving by asking yourself the following questions: Do other drivers honk at you frequently? Is nighttime or highway driving stressful to you? Do other cars seem to appear out of nowhere? Are the breaks in traffic hard for you to gauge? Are sharp turns becoming tricky?

1. Monitor your eyesight through regular professional exams. Most of the cues you get while driving are visual. Vision declines with age. Be aware of what you can and can't see. Don't rely on the eye exam given during your license renewal. Passing it does not mean that your sight is problem-free.
2. Many prescription and over-the-counter drugs can inhibit your ability to drive a car. Be careful of taking

more than one prescription at a time. Ask your physician or pharmacist to review your medicines, and, if necessary, alter the mix to lessen the impact on your driving.

3. The most important thing you can do is work around, not against, your limitations. Often there are things you can do to compensate for your driving difficulties. If necessary, avoid rush-hour or nighttime driving, and take side roads instead of busy highways.

4. Your car may also have its own limitations. Make certain that you have a good view of the road from the driver's seat. If you no longer have a good view of the road, it may be time to make adjustments or buy a different car. When you buy a car, look for a model with these features: doors that open wide, a floor with a low step-in height, trunks and hoods that are simple to open and close, comfortable seat belts with shoulder-height adjustment, controls that are boldly numbered and easy to reach and use, and large, glare-control rear-view mirrors that dim automatically.

5 THINGS TO ASK A DOCTOR BEFORE YOU TRAVEL

Not every clinic or doctor providing travel medicine is competent. To make certain that you are getting quality travel medicine services, there are five things you should do.

1. Ask for the name of the travel physician over the phone, as well as his or her background and training. Travel physicians are frequently trained in the areas of internal medicine, family practice, and emergency medicine. To determine if the physician is board certified, consult the *Directory of Medical Specialists* available at most public libraries.

2. Request information by fax or recorded message from the Centers for Disease Control (CDC) Traveler's Hotline on vaccine recommendations for specified areas, disease risks, and preventive health measures. The telephone service is available at 404-639-2572. Use the CDC's suggestions as a starting point. Getting the best medical advice for an overseas trip is not as easy as going to a book or calling a hotline. Information in a book may be dated, incomplete, or not applicable to your health situation.

3. Get the best advice and immunizations you can by going to competent travel clinics. Expect and ask for a variety of information and printed material from the doctor you go to. Some clinics even issue a report customized for each country on the itinerary.

4. Travel medicine providers should also ask you about any underlying health problems and inquire about your specific travel plans. A business traveler may have different risks than a person exploring rural areas.

5. Above all, take the time to get the proper immunizations before traveling overseas. Doing so can be your first step to an enjoyable vacation.

5 ARTHRITIS GETAWAY TIPS

Don't let arthritis pain slow down your next vacation. The following tips can make the difference in helping you get the most out of your getaway.

1. Select a hotel that has accommodations, such as ramps and bathtub handrails, that allow you to move around easily. A heated pool or spa for exercising and relaxing is a plus.

2. Pack lightly and use a suitcase with wheels.

3. Pack any medication you are going to need in your carry-on bag and not in your check-in luggage. Don't forget to bring along needed over-the-counter medication in case it is not readily available at your final destination.

4. Stretching can keep your joints from becoming stiff. Simple stretching can be done even in flight. Make sure to get up and walk around several times during a long flight. Once you are at your hotel, daily exercise, such as swimming or walking, can reduce the pain of arthritis.

5. Above all, take time to relax. Overdoing physical activity is the fastest way to end up in pain. Read a good book, take a bus tour, or just sit and soak up the scenery.

5 TIPS FOR MORE COMFORTABLE COACH SEATING

When you book a coach seat for a flight, you expect cramped seating, but the following tips can make a world of differences in your travel comfort.

1. On a wide-body plane, request an aisle seat in the center section. Middle seats are considered the least desirable and therefore are the last assigned.
2. If the majority of the seats on your plane are in groups of three, one member of a couple is usually assigned the middle seat. Couples should ask for a window and an aisle seat. There is a good chance that the middle seat will then be one of the last assigned.
3. Many airlines reserve a section in coach for members of their frequent-flier programs. Those airlines say they assign middle seats in those sections only when the planes are full. If you're a frequent flier, that's a big advantage. But if you're not, your odds of sitting next to an occupied middle seat increase.
    Certain seats have more legroom than others. There are particular seats you may want to request. Remember, if you sit next to an exit door, you are required to be able to physically perform certain procedures in case of an emergency.
4. Most wide-body planes have exit doors in the middle of the cabin and the rows directly behind these doors have extra legroom.
5. If you sit right behind a cabin divider, you may get extra legroom and nobody can sit in front of you.

8 EMERGENCY FLYING TIPS

1. **Book an aisle seat.** It gives you an added advantage when exiting in an emergency situation.
2. **Ask for a seat close to an exit.** Know exactly where that exit is and count how many rows away it is in case of a blackout. Also, have a second exit in mind.
3. **Buy a seat for your baby.** Usually, everything on a plane is secured except babies. Although not required, parents should consider buying a separate seat for children under the age of two and bringing an approved child-restraint seat on board.
4. **Wear sneakers or low, rubber-heeled shoes.** If it becomes necessary, you want to be able to get out of the plane in a hurry.
5. **Don't load heavy or odd-shaped luggage in the overhead compartment above you.** The compartments can pop open and the contents can come crashing down on you.
6. **Pay attention to the safety demonstration.** Always pay attention and read the safety card. Every plane is different.
7. **Keep exits accessible.** Place all tray tables in the upright position and keep the aisle in front of your feet clear. Keep books, magazines, blankets, pillows, and so forth, out of your escape path.
8. **Stay alert.** Don't let alcohol or drugs (over-the-counter or otherwise) hinder your awareness.

11 TRAVEL TIPS FOR THOSE WITH DISABILITIES

Over 40 million Americans have disabilities. The Air Carrier Access Act and the Department of Transportation (DOT) rule set out procedures designed to ensure that these Americans have the same opportunity as anyone else to enjoy a pleasant trip. Here are some of the major provisions of the rule.

1. Except in certain limited circumstances, a person may not be refused transportation on the basis of disability or be required to have an attendant or produce a medical certificate.

2. Airlines must provide enplaning, deplaning, and connecting assistance. Some small commuter aircraft may not be accessible to passengers with severe mobility impairments. (If you are flying to a small city, ask ahead of time about plane size, available assistance, and other pertinent information.)

3. Airport terminals and airline reservations centers must have TDD (Telecommunications Device for the Deaf) telephone devices for persons with hearing or speech impairments.

4. Passengers with vision or hearing impairments must have timely access to the same information given to other passengers at the airport and on the plane concerning gate assignments, delayed flights, safety, and so forth.

5. New wide-body aircraft must have a wheelchair-accessible lavatory and an on-board wheelchair. On

most other flights, an airline must place a wheelchair on board upon request.

6. Air carriers must accept wheelchairs as checked baggage and cannot require passengers to sign liability waivers for them.

7. Most new airplanes must have movable armrests on at least half of the aisle seats and on-board stowage for one folding wheelchair.

8. Although most exit rows on planes have more room, Federal Aviation Administration (FAA) safety rules establish standards for passengers who are sitting in emergency exit rows. People in these rows must be able to fully perform certain evacuation-related procedures.

9. FAA rules prohibit passengers from bringing their own oxygen on board. Although not required, most airlines will provide aircraft-approved oxygen for a fee.

10. Airlines may not charge for any services that are required by the Air Carrier Access Act and DOT rule.

11. Airlines must make available a specially trained complaints resolution official if a dispute arises.

12 SYMPTOMS TO ALERT YOU TO TRAVEL SCAMS

Unlike most goods and services, travel services are usually paid for in advance. This creates opportunities for disreputable individuals and companies to take advantage of unsuspecting customers. Some travel packages turn out to be very different from what was presented or expected. Some don't materialize at all!

If you receive an unsolicited offer by phone or mail for a free or extremely low-priced vacation trip to a popular destination (often Hawaii or Florida), be alert. Here are some questions to ask yourself:

1. Does the price seem too good to be true? If so, it probably is.
2. Are you required to give your credit card number over the phone?
3. Are you pressured to make an immediate decision?
4. Is the airline clearly identified, or does the representative give you a number of different airlines without being able to say which one you will be flying on?
5. Is the representative unable or unwilling to give you a street address for his or her company?
6. Are you told you can't leave for at least two months? (The deadline for disputing a credit card charge is 60 days. Most scam artists know this and will thus delay your departure date.)
7. If you are told that you've won a free vacation, ask if you have to buy something else in order to get it. If you do, be suspicious and proceed with extreme caution. If the trip is supposedly "free," it shouldn't cost you anything.
8. If you are seriously considering the vacation offer and are confident you have established the full price you will pay, compare the offer to what you might obtain elsewhere. The appeal of "free" airfare or free accommodations often hides the fact that the total price may

still be higher than that of a respectable package tour that offers the same things.

9. Get a confirmed departure date in writing before you pay *anything*. View skeptically any promises that an "acceptable date" will be arranged later.

10. If the destination is a beach resort, ask how far the hotel is from the beach. Then call the hotel to verify.

11. Determine the complete cost of the trip in dollars, including all service charges, taxes, and processing fees.

12. If you decide to buy the trip after checking it out, paying by credit card gives you certain legal rights to pursue a chargeback (credit) if promised services aren't delivered.

If you encounter any of these symptoms, proceed cautiously. Ask for written information to be sent to you. A legitimate travel company will be happy to oblige. If they don't have a brochure, ask for a day or two to think it over; most bona fide deals that are good today will still be good two days from now. If they say no to both requests, this probably isn't the trip for you.

ADVICE FOR PASSPORT RENEWALS

If you're renewing a passport or applying for a visa by mail, the State Department suggests using a padded envelope because regular envelopes can tear when they're being processed at the post office. Travelers should include a current return address inside their passport so that if the document becomes separated from the envelope, it can still be returned.

A COSTLY MISTAKE

Hotel cancellation fees are charged by some hotels if guaranteed reservations are canceled less than 72 hours before a scheduled arrival. A traveler whose plans change at the last minute may be charged for one night's stay. Such penalties are standard at many resort properties but are now spreading to business hotels in major cities. Some hotels are also charging penalties to guests who check out earlier than expected. Always make sure to find out the hotel's policies when making your reservations.

EUROPEAN CAR RENTAL

When renting cars in Europe, keep in mind that the least expensive models are usually small and are likely to have stick shifts. A car advertised as a four-seater may be suitable for only two adults and two children, not four adults, and luggage space may be severely limited. Instead of specifying the class of car, tell the rental agent how many people will be in the car and how much luggage you will be carrying.

MEDICAL INSURANCE

Some insurance companies may not pay medical claims incurred outside the United States. If your company does not cover care in foreign countries, you may want to purchase extended trip coverage. You can also buy insurance to cover medical evacuation, lost bags, and trip interruptions.

MUMBO JUMBO YOU SHOULD KNOW

Like other specialized professions, the hotel industry has developed its own lingo for doing business. To make certain you get a fair shake when dealing with hotel managers and reservation agents, it's important that you understand some of the terms used in the industry.

Being Walked: When you arrive with a reservation and the clerk informs you that the hotel is overbooked and your reservation has been moved to another hotel, you've been "walked." There's not much you can do except insist on the industry's standard make-good offer of a free phone call or two and the first night's lodging free.

Continental Breakfast: This term can be applied to a variety of spreads. To make sure your "breakfast" is more than a cold cup of coffee and a stale pastry, call your hotel ahead of time and ask for the specifics.

Diamonds: These gems are part of the five-point rating system from the American Automobile Association (AAA). Hotels are rated according to the quality of their facilities and service, with five diamonds denoting the highest.

Occupancy Rates: These rates vary widely by area and season. Nationwide, year-round rates are about 70 percent. Hotels that participate in discount programs usually don't offer their best bargains unless the hotel expects to be less than 80 percent full.

Rack Rates: Short for "off the rack." This term refers to the first rate a reservation agent will quote you when you call and ask about rates. But it's possible for almost anyone to get a lower rate than the first one quoted. Start by inquiring about weekend promotions or special rates for business travelers or members of large organizations, like AAA. Lower rates often apply to government employees and employees of large companies as well. Credit card companies are also involved in several hotel promotions, so be sure and ask if there are any. Regardless of what available rate you are quoted, it's always important to inquire about any special discounts and promotions.

Stars: Foreign governments use the star system to rate hotels in their countries. Five stars is usually the top. Beware of hotels outside the United States advertising themselves as four-star establishments. Many may have never been evaluated by an unbiased observer. Government star-rating programs, such as those in France and Italy, usually focus more on the facilities than on the service, location, and design.

These programs also tend to pay more attention to public areas than to private rooms.

Suite: A hotel suite is a unit with a bedroom and a separate living area. But over the last ten years, hotels have taken to calling many of their units suites, when in reality it is only a bedroom with room for a love seat. Ask if it is a true suite or a divided room.

PUT MORE GREEN (OR YELLOW OR RED OR BLUE) IN YOUR POCKET

Would you like to obtain money overseas without standing in long lines or paying an overinflated exchange rate at the local bank? It's easier than you think. Increasingly advanced technology and a fiercely competitive travel and financial environment have given you a number of simple, safe, and economical money-changing alternatives to the old stand-bys, traveler's checks and cash. While both traveler's checks and cash are good options when traveling abroad, there are other options.

- In most places you can get local foreign currency the same way you get your greenbacks here—at your friendly, local ATM (Automated Teller Machine). Using an ATM card to obtain money is not only convenient, it's cost effective. In a recent survey sponsored by Visa, using a U.S.-issued card at a foreign ATM was found to be 43 percent less expensive than

exchanging money at a foreign airport, and 53 percent less expensive than exchanging currency at
hotels. But heed this advice about taking the ATM
route. First, always check with your bank about any
daily withdrawal limits it may have on your ATM card
and, if needed, get the limit raised. Also, most
machines abroad use a four-digit PIN; if your PIN is
not four digits, contact your bank for an alternate
number. Call Phone Plus at 1-800-491-1145 or Cirrus
at 1-800-4-CIRRUS to inquire about ATM locations
around the world.

- If you can't find an ATM, or if a machine won't accept
  your ATM card, a credit card is an excellent alternative. You can obtain a cash advance on your Visa or
  MasterCard at banks and ATMs. You get an advantageous commercial rate and you can take only the
  amount of money you need. But be aware that in
  most cases you pay a cash advance fee and a small
  percentage (usually, 1 or 2 percent up to a maximum
  of $10 to $25) of your transaction for a foreign currency conversion fee. And cash advances may begin
  accruing finance charges right away.

- Check cards, also called debit cards or money cards,
  are a popular alternative to credit cards. The Visa
  Check Card and MasterCard's Master Money are the
  most popular cards. They are accepted wherever Visa
  or MasterCard is accepted, but rather than drawing
  on your line of credit, these cards take money

directly out of your bank checking account without the paperwork or identification hassles. Many travelers who don't want to pay interest on a charge-card balance prefer the check card option.

3 QUESTIONS TO ASK YOUR BANKER ABOUT YOUR ATM CARD

1. In the places I'm visiting, where can I find the ATMs that accept my card? (That's a question usually answered in a folder available from your bank listing all your ATM system's overseas locations.)
2. What is the fee for an overseas withdrawal?
3. Does my card need to be modified to work overseas? (That query should elicit an offer from the bank to modify its magnetic imprint, if need be.)

SUITABLE SUITCASE TIPS

Suitcase manufacturers are working on new designs to make traveling easier on the back and other injury-prone areas of the body. New designs include a square suitcase instead of the traditional rectangular design. The square shape lowers the center of gravity on the suitcase and makes it less likely to tip over. Other innovations include a four-wheel base, locating the wheels at the bag's corners instead of tucked underneath toward the center, and a U-shaped pull bar anchored to each side of the suitcase frame. In general, travelers should use suitcases with straps or wheels instead of traditional models with handles. In addition, travelers should use backpacks whenever possible to reduce the risk of injury to the back and hands. Side compartments on a suitcase afford easy access to contents and can also reduce the risk of pain by minimizing the picking up and putting down of suitcases while traveling.

TRAVEL ALERT

Never openly display your name and address on luggage tags. Burglars linger in check-in areas and luggage carousels looking for leads on people who won't be home. They also get leads from magazines you bring from home, so tear off the labels with your address.

TRAVEL TIP

Get a detailed itinerary from your travel agent when picking up your tickets. Put one copy in your carry-on bag. Put another copy inside your suitcase on top of your clothes. If your suitcase is lost, the itinerary makes it easier for the carrier to return it to you. Leave a third copy with your family or others so they know where you can be reached in case of an emergency.

TRAVEL RESOURCES

FABULOUS FACTORY TOURS

Hershey's in Oakdale, California, is not as well known as the Pennsylvania headquarters, but it offers a better look at candy making. Hershey's Kisses and Reese's Peanut Butter Cups are made here, and the aroma alone is worth the trip. Receive a FREE candy bar or 10 percent off a gift-shop item as part of your tour. **For more information, phone (209) 848-8126.**

E-One in Ocala, Florida, manufactures every variety of fire engines used in many towns and cities. Its factory is full of the sound of sirens being tested, the dance of welder's sparks and 1,200 different shades of fire-engine-red paint. In addition, you will receive a FREE cap with logo and the chance to sit in the driver's seat of a new fire engine. **For more information, phone (904) 237-1122.**

Ben & Jerry's Ice Cream Factory in Waterbury, Vermont, cranks out 180,000 pints a day. From tank room to flavor vat, chunk feeder to spiral hardener, you'll see it all from above while a guide explains the operation. Enjoy the FREE flavor samples. **For more information, phone (802) 244-8687.**

Boeing in Everett, Washington, is the world's largest aircraft company and builds some of the largest airplanes in the world's largest building. It covers 98 acres. You'll see 747s from

35 feet above the assembly floor and 767s and 777s on the flight line. Children must be at least 45 inches tall from their toes to the bridge of their nose to take this tour. **For more information, phone (202) 544-1264.**

U.S. BUREAU OF ENGRAVING AND PRINTING ALLOWANCE in Washington, D.C., is where our paper money and stamps are printed. The spectacle is mind-boggling. From an overhead walkway, much of the production process is visible. **For more information, phone (202) 874-3019.**

FUN AND WACKY FESTIVALS

THE CALAVERAS COUNTY FAIR and Jumping Frog Jubilee is held the third weekend in May at Angels Camp, California. Mark Twain was inspired by Angels Camp's celebrated jumping frogs to write that famous short story. Continue the tradition by entering a frog (your own or a rental) in the contest that highlights this annual county fair. **For more information, phone (209) 736-2561.**

THE GILROY GARLIC FESTIVAL is held the last weekend in July in Gilroy, California. Garlic has been used for centuries as an antibiotic, as a means to ward off.vampires and as an essential ingredient in spaghetti sauce. Find garlic in places you'd never expect: gum, tea, cantaloupe, jelly, and ice cream. The festival also features music, garlic-braiding classes, and arts and crafts. **For more information, phone (408) 842-1625.**

THE POPEYE PICNIC is held annually at the beginning of September in Chester, Illinois. Attend the annual meeting of the Popeye Fan Club or just browse in the Popeye Museum. Enjoy the parade, fireworks, 10K race, craft show, and more. **For more information, phone 1-800-782-9587, or for Popeye fan club information, phone (618) 826-4567.**

THE WORLD CHAMPIONSHIP COW CHIP THROWING CONTEST, held in April, will bring Beaver, Oklahoma, to the attention of the sports world. Each autumn, early settlers filled their wagons with cow chips and tossing chips into the wagon became great sport. Today, contestants compete to see who can throw them the farthest. A carnival, a chuck wagon feed, a stock-car race, concerts, and more round out the festivities. **For more information, phone (405) 625-4726.**

THE MOUNT HOREB MUSTARD MUSEUM is a must for those of us who relish this condiment. The museum was founded by the former assistant district attorney of Wisconsin. The museum has 2,286 different kinds of mustard on display and is open from 10 A.M. to 5 P.M. daily. **For more information, write to Mount Horeb Mustard Museum, P.O. Box 468, Mount Horeb, WI 53572; or phone (608) 437-3986.**

LAST-MINUTE TRAVEL SAVES YOU A BUNDLE

It's possible for you to enjoy considerable travel savings—often as much as 60 percent! For example, if you want to take a cruise to Cancun, Mexico, it may cost about $929 for a week. Wait three or four weeks before departure and you might be able to get the same package for a scant $199! Contact:

SPUR-OF-THE-MOMENT CRUISES sells berths for 30–50 percent less than "brochure rates" for cruises departing one week to three months after you call (the service is FREE). **For more information, phone 1-800-343-1991.**

ENCORE TRAVEL CLUB offers a 30-day FREE trial and charges $49 per year for its directory guaranteeing 50 percent off hotel rates, up to 30 percent off car rentals, and other offers. Reservations can be made no more than 30 days and no less than 48 hours in advance. **For more information, phone 1-800-638-0930.**

MOMENT'S NOTICE charges $25 per year. Subscribers use a special phone number to access a prerecorded message (updated daily) that lists bargain packages to the Caribbean and Mexico, as well as cruises and airfares to Europe—all due to depart within 2 to 30 days. **For more information, phone (212) 486-0500.**

THE ROOM EXCHANGE brokers leftover space—20–50 percent off regular rates—at more than 22,000 hotels in the United States, Canada, and the Caribbean. While last-minute discounts are prevalent, you can also save big on some bookings made in advance. **For more information, phone 1-800-846-7000, 9 A.M. to 5 P.M. EST**. Simply reserve and pay by credit card over the phone.

1-800-FLY-ASAP (that's the name and the phone number) offers bargains on last-minute airline travel in the United States and to Canada, Mexico, and the Caribbean. The company's $6 fee covers ticket delivery. **For more information, phone 1-800-FLY-ASAP.**

LODGING AND DINING SAVINGS

TASTE PUBLICATIONS runs a popular program that offers savings on dining entertainment and accommodations. "America at a Discount," $19.95 yearly, offers savings of up to 25 percent or more on rack rates at participating hotels, discounted meals at selected locations, and reduced-price movie passes (offered by mail for United Artists, Loews, and theaters in other major cities). **For more information, write to Taste Publications International, 1031 Cromwell Bridge Rd., Baltimore, MD 21202; phone 1-800-248-2783 or (410) 825-3463.**

GREAT AMERICAN TRAVELER offers discounts at some 1,500 hotels nationwide. Membership is $22.95, but for $20 more you can upgrade to the "Golf Access" membership, which features 50 percent discounts on courses in North America, among other benefits. **For more information, write to Colonial Vacations, 1945 Hoover Ct., Birmingham, AL 35226; phone 1-800-548-2812; fax (205) 979-1038.**

INTERNATIONAL TRAVEL CARD, also known as ITC, costs $36 a year and features savings of up to 50 percent on over 1,500 hotels nationwide. **For more information, write to ITC, 6001 N. Clark St., Chicago, IL 60660; or phone 1-800-477-3234 or 1-800-285-5525.**

LONG-DISTANCE HOME SWAP

As hotel rates climb, many travelers are becoming involved in home exchanges. But before a traveler decides to exchange homes with another, both parties should make certain that they understand each other and each other's properties. Early on, "swappers" should agree on how to handle a cancellation. You should also make sure your homeowners' insurance covers major damage that may be caused by a house-exchange visitor and covers liability if an exchanger is injured inside your house. Make sure to leave your home clean, providing clean linens for your guests, as well as directions to the nearest grocery store, an emergency room, and any other locations you feel are important. If you're trading cars, too, make sure the tank is full and your car insurance is in order. Also, leave phone numbers of trusted friends in case of an emergency, and agree on how to handle long-distance phone bills and replacement of any items broken. And if any room is off-limits, clearly specify it as such.

Below is a list of companies specializing in home exchanging.

HOME EXCHANGE NETWORK is an electronic site, founded in November 1993. Internet address: www.magicnet.net/home-xchange. The list carries 400–500 homes daily, about 80 percent of them in the United States. A year's membership costs $29.95 and allows you to list up to two homes. **For additional information, write to Box 951253, Longwood, FL 32791; or phone (407) 862-5956.**

INTERVAC U.S. is the U.S. link of an international group of affiliated companies founded in 1953. Intervac, "the largest home exchange in the world," publishes four catalogs yearly and charges $78 for a year's membership, $11 more to include a photo with a listing. Seniors get $5 off. Catalogues list about 10,000 homes yearly, most in Europe, with 205 in the United States. **For more information, write to Box 590504, San Francisco, CA 94159; or phone 1-800-756-4663 or (415) 435-3497; fax (415) 435-7440.**

THE INVENTED CITY, founded in 1991, sends out three directories yearly. Proprietor Glenn London charges $50 for a year's membership ($60 if you include a photo) and boasts membership of about 2,000 households in 15–20 countries. **For more information, write to 41 Sutter St., Suite 1090, San Francisco, CA 94109; or phone 1-800-788-2489 or (415) 673-0347; fax (415) 673-6909.**

TEACHER SWAP was founded in 1986 by a Long Island, New York, high school English teacher. An annual directory goes out each March with supplements in April and June. Membership (including one directory listing and copies of one directory and the two supplements) runs $42 a year. **For more information write to Box 454, Oakdale, NY 11769; or phone (516) 244-2845.**

TRADING HOMES INTERNATIONAL, based in Hermosa Beach, California, sends out directories in March, June, and December every year and is linked with 15 worldwide exchange organizations worldwide. An estimated 2,000 homes are listed in the course of a year, about half in North America and 25–30 percent in Europe. For a $65 one-year membership, a swapper gets listed in one directory and receives copies of three. About three of every four listings include photographs. **For more information, write to P.O. Box 787, Hermosa Beach, CA 90254; or phone 1-800-877-8723 or (310) 798-3864; fax (310) 798-3865.**

MUSICAL MUSEUM TOUR

THE LAWRENCE WELK MUSEUM features a model of a bandstand with life-size cardboard cutouts of Welk. You can stand beside the bubbly bandleader and, through the magic of a TV monitor, imagine you're a guest. The museum also serves as the lobby of a 330-seat musical theater. **The Lawrence Welk Museum is located at 8845 Lawrence Welk Dr., Escondido, California.**

THE HOUSE OF CASH proves once and for all that if a prize were offered for the star receiving the most gifts from prison inmates, Johnny Cash would win hands down. In his museum, a whole section has been devoted to men behind bars who've sent mementos, such as a ball and chain, metal cups, and a church made of glued gravel. **The House of Cash is located on Star Route 31E, Hendersonville, Tennessee.**

THE DELTA BLUES MUSEUM is home to recordings, photos and other memorabilia of such blues greats as W. C. Handy and Muddy Waters. Vintage instruments include a turn-of-the-century leather-head banjo and a collection tracing the origins of the blues guitar. **The Delta Blues Museum is located 70 miles south of Memphis at 114 Delta Ave., Clarksdale, Mississippi.**

THE MUSIC HOUSE is a 6,000-square-foot replica of a turn-of-the-century village exhibiting mechanical instruments, including a huge Mortier dance organ. It was built in 1922 for the Victorian Palace in southern Belgium to resemble the sound of a 30-piece dance orchestra. One gallery shows the development of the radio, phonograph, and jukebox. **The Music House is located at 7377 U.S. 31 N., Acme, Michigan.**

THE CLEVELAND ROCK AND ROLL HALL OF FAME AND MUSEUM is home to Buddy Holly's high school diploma, John Lennon's Sgt. Pepper jacket, and Elvis Presley's guitar, among other priceless items. The $92 million, 150,000 square-foot facility on the shores of Lake Erie is billed as the world's first museum dedicated to the living heritage of rock and roll music. It is packed with musical memorabilia and also has outdoor and indoor performance spaces, working studios and interactive exhibits. **The Rock and Roll Hall of Fame and Museum is located at 1 Key Plaza, Cleveland, OH 44114.**

PARKING IT

For general information about our national parks, contact the **Office of Public Inquiries, National Park Service, Box 32127, Room 1013, Washington, DC 20013; or phone (202) 208-4747.**

Seniors over 62 qualify for a $10 Golden Age Passport admitting them and a carful of relatives or friends to any park.

WHAT THE TOP EIGHT
TRAVEL CLUBS OFFER

AMERICA AT A DISCOUNT ($19.95 yearly). Discounts of 50 percent at 1,400 U.S. hotels and up to 50 percent at chains (2,500 hotels). Also up to 65 percent off weekly stays in vacation condos in the United States, Mexico, and the Caribbean; up to 25 percent off car rentals; up to 40 percent off cruises; 25 percent off restaurants; and a 5 percent air travel rebate; **phone 1-800-248-2783.**

ENTERTAINMENT PUBLICATIONS. A series of 124 value-packed travel directories with more than 75,000 participating merchants, including Travel America at HalfPrice ($32.95); HalfPrice Europe ($42); 119 city editions in the United States and Canada ($25 to $45); and editions for Israel and London ($41.95 each); **phone 1-800-285-5525.**

INTERNATIONAL TRAVEL CARD ($36). Discounts of 50 percent at 2,500 worldwide hotels are listed; **phone 1-800-342-0558.**

QUEST INTERNATIONAL ($99). Fifty percent off at more than 2,000 hotels in the United States, Caribbean, Mexico, Canada, and Europe; also 50 percent off vacation condos and cruises; **phone 1-800-325-2400.**

SEE AMERICA. This club offers the International Golf Directory ($49.94) and See America at 50% Discount ($99.95), a directory of 1,500 hotels in the United States, Canada, Mexico, and New Zealand; **phone (410) 653-2616.**

SOLID GOLD ($42). Up to 50 percent off at 400 hotels in Canada and the United States, plus discounts at Canadian restaurants, parks, and auto services; **phone (604) 689-4440.**

TRAVEL WORLD LEISURE CLUB ($50). Discounts of up to 30 percent at restaurants and hotels, 25 percent on rental cars and 14 major cruise lines, and 5–40 percent on airfares; **phone 1-800-444-8952.**

DISCOUNTS: PLANES, TRAINS, HOTELS, OH MY!

Most airlines offer a 10 percent discount for people age 62 or older. Below are savings in addition to the standard discount. Make sure to ask for your discount when inquiring about and when making your reservation. Also, remember to ask about any restrictions, blackout dates, and proof-of-age requirements.

DOMESTIC CARRIERS

AMERICAN AIRLINES
Senior SAAver Club, Senior TrAAveler Coupon Books; **phone 1-800-433-7300**

CONTINENTAL AIRLINES
Year-long Freedom Passport, Freedom Trips Coupon Books, various senior discounts
Freedom Passport; **phone 1-800-441-1135**
Freedom Trips: **phone 1-800-248-8996**

DELTA AIRLINES
Young at Heart Coupon Books; **phone 1-800-221-1212**

NORTHWEST AIRLINES
World Perks Senior, Free Travel Club, Ultrafare Coupon Books; **phone 1-800-225-2525**

UNITED AIRLINES
Silver Wings Plus (over 60) Club, Silver Travel Pac Coupon Books, 10 percent discount on United Airlines, United Express, Iberia, KLM, Sabena, and Alitalia flights for folks over 62; **phone 1-800-628-2868**

FOREIGN CARRIERS

BRITISH AIRWAYS
10 percent discount, privileged traveler card for 60+, companions 50+ get same discount; **phone 1-800-247-9297**

KLM ROYAL DUTCH

Those over 60 (and spouses of any age get a discount to Tel Aviv from New York in off season, 10 percent discount if you're over 62 and a member of United's Silver Wings Plus Program; **phone 1-800-777-5553**

MEXICANA AIRLINES

10 percent discount for you and a companion of any age; **phone 1-800-531-7921**

TAP AIR PORTUGAL

Off-season (September through May) discounts for travelers over 60 and their companions; **phone 1-800-221-7370**

TRAINS

AMTRAK

Travelers over 62 receive 15 percent discount on the lowest available round-trip coach fares. Blackouts occur during major holidays, Friday–Sunday. Buy tickets in advance; **phone 1-800-872-7425**

BRITISH TOURIST AUTHORITY

Travelers over 60 get a 15-day BritRail Senior Pass for unlimited travel in England, Scotland, and Wales ($455 for first class, $305 economy). Buy in the United States, not sold in Britain, valid in first class and standard class (Note: Eurailpass not valid in Great Britain); write Britrail, 1500 Broadway, New York, NY 10036; **phone 1-800-677-8585**

EUROPEAN RAILROAD PASSES

Entitles you to 30–50 percent discount off the normal rail fare throughout Europe for a year. You also receive discounts on many ferries and private railroads; write Eurailpass, Box 325, Old Greenwich, CT 06870-0325; **phone 1-800-421-2999**

BUSES

GRAY LINE TOURS
AARP members and members of other Senior Clubs (50 years or older) are eligible for 15 percent discount on half-day and full-day sight-seeing tours. Members of other groups may also qualify. You must buy your ticket at the terminal office in order to receive the discount; **phone Gray Line Tours at 1-800-583-5900**

VOYAGEUR
Club 60 discounts by 33 percent regular fares on regular bus service in Ontario and Quebec and provinces daily except Friday and Sunday (25 percent), show proof of age (60 or older) at time of ticket purchase, frequent travelers: $159 plus tax; 10-day tour pass (between May 1 and October 15) available for unlimited travels on Voyageur, plus 47 other carriers in Ontario and Quebec; **phone Voyageur at (416) 393-7911**

CAR RENTALS

Shown below are car rental companies that offer discounts to members of many senior citizen groups. Among the most popular groups are AARP, CARP (Canadian Association of Retired Persons), airline senior citizens clubs, and hotel senior citizens clubs. Ask about receiving a discount through any senior citizens organization to which you may belong.

ALAMO
phone 1-800-327-9633

AVIS
phone 1-800-331-1212

DOLLAR
phone 1-800-800-4000

HERTZ
AARP or Mature Outlook members get 15–20 percent discounts, 10–25 percent discount on time and mileage rates at many locations; **phone 1-800-654-3131**

KEMWEL
phone 1-800-678-0678

NATIONAL
AARP members get a $32 daily flat rate; 10 percent weekly and weekend rate discount, 10 percent daily rate discount for some overseas rentals; **phone 1-800-CAR-RENT**

THRIFTY RENT-A-CAR
AARP members enjoy a 10 percent discount off almost any rate Thrifty offers in the United States and Canada; **phone 1-800-367-2277**

HOTELS

Hotels, like airlines, offer lots of different discounts, many for the over-50 crowd. A sampling is listed below. If possible, call the hotel you want to stay at and ask for their lowest listed price. The rates you'll get are usually cheaper than the rates you get from the 800 number. Many hotels require that you make your reservations in advance to get the discount. Make sure you mention your senior discount at the time you make your reservation.

BEST WESTERN INTERNATIONAL

Travelers over 55 get a 10 percent discount at most of the 2,000 hotels and motor inns in the United States and Canada; **For a FREE copy of the Best Western Travel Guide, write Best Western International, 6201 N. 24th Pkwy., Phoenix, AZ 85016; phone 1-800-528-1234 or 1-800-528-2222 for the hearing impaired.**

CHOICE HOTEL INTERNATIONAL

CHOICE HOTEL INTERNATIONAL (Sleep Inn, Comfort, Quality, Clarion, Friendship Inn, Econo Lodge, and Rodeway hotels and resorts) Prime Time program for people age 50 and older, or to card-carrying members of a senior citizen organization, 10 percent discount on room rates; **For information and reservations, phone 1-800-221-2222, 1-800-228-3323 for the hearing impaired.**

DAYS INNS

September Days Club membership offers 15–50 percent discounts to people over 50, 10 percent discount on meals and gifts at participating locations and a variety of other discount and special services. Spouses of all ages get membership privileges at no extra cost. Membership dues are $12 annually. **For membership information, phone 1-800-241-5050; for reservations phone 1-800-247-5152 or 1-800-222-3297 for the hearing impaired.**

DOUBLETREE CLUB

Seniors receive 15 percent off published rates; **phone 1-800-522-0444.**

DRURY INNS
Travelers 50 or over receive a 10 percent discount on room rate; **phone 1-800-325-8300.**

ECONOMY INNS OF AMERICA
Room rates reduced by 10 percent for those over 55; **phone 1-800-826-0778.**

EMBASSY SUITES
Offers a 10 percent discount on two-room suite with kitchenette, AAA and AARP members eligible for discount as well as members of the National Council of Senior Citizens and the National Retired Teachers Association. Holders of Silver Savers Passports qualify for discounts at some locations; **phone 1-800-372-2779.**

HAMPTON INNS
Lifestyle 50 provides savings for guests over 50; **phone 1-800-426-7866.**

HILTON
Senior Honors Club offers travelers over 60 (55, if retired) room discounts of up to 50 percent off, preferred rates and discounts from Hertz, 20 percent discounts on dinners at Hilton restaurants, and special customer services. Lifetime worldwide fee of $284 or $65 per year, $50/year for domestic only. Rates are slightly higher for nonresidents of the United States. A $25 certificate is issued for each $300 charge (Note: When registering for the club, fill out a "guest preference profile" so all Hilton Hotels will know your special needs and preferences in advance); **phone 1-800-492-3232.**

HOLIDAY INN

Preferred Seniors program gives 20 percent discount on room rates to members of any national senior citizens program, 10 percent discount at Holiday Inn restaurants, discounts on Hertz and National rental cars; **phone 1-800-465-4329.**

HYATT HOTELS

Participating hotels discount rates starting at 10 percent; **phone 1-800-842-4242.**

LA QUINTA INN

Offers a 10 percent discount for those 55 or over, or to members of seniors organizations; **phone 1-800-531-5900.**

RADISSON HOTELS

Those 50 or over are entitled to approximately 25 percent off regular rates, AARP members may also receive a 15 percent discount in certain Radisson restaurants and lounges; **phone 1-800-282-5711.**

RAMADA INTERNATIONAL HOTELS AND RESORTS

Participating Ramadas offer 25 percent off applicable room rates to mature travelers age 60 and over or members of the organizations listed below: AARP, the Golden Buckeye Club, and the National Council of Senior Citizens; **phone 1-800-228-3232.**

RED LION HOTELS AND INNS

Regular rates reduced 20 percent for lodgers over 50 belonging to AARP or Mature Overlook or holding Silver Savers Passports cards. Also, 10 percent off regular menu in most Red Lion restaurants (not valid on holidays); **phone 1-800-547-8010.**

Red Roof Inns
Redi Card over-60 members get a 10 percent discount plus special privileges; $10 fee for lifetime membership; **phone 1-800-843-7663.**

Travelodge
Fifteen percent discounts available to Travelodge's FREE Classic Travel Club or AARP members; **phone 1-800-255-3050.**

Vagabond Inns
Club 55 membership for travelers over 55 offers discount coupons good toward stays at any Vagabond Inn; **phone 1-800-522-1555.**

FOREIGN TOURIST OFFICES

The following tourist offices offer information to the public on visiting their countries.

ALBERTA TOURISM
10147 Canyonridge Place
Spring Valley, CA 91977
(619) 466-0321
Fax (619) 466-0321

AUSTRIAN NATIONAL
 TOURIST OFFICE
P.O. Box 491938
Los Angeles, CA 90049
(310) 477-3332
Fax (310) 477-5141

AUSTRIAN NATIONAL
 TOURIST OFFICE
500 Fifth Ave. #2009
New York, NY 10110
(212) 944-6880

BAHAMAS TOURIST OFFICE
3450 Wilshire Blvd. #208
Los Angeles, CA 90010
1-800-422-4262
Fax (213) 383-3966

BELGIAN TOURIST OFFICE
780 Third Ave. #1501
New York, NY 10017
(212) 758-8130

BERMUDA DEPARTMENT
OF TOURISM
3151 Cahuenga Blvd. West #111
Los Angeles, CA 90068
(213) 436-0744
Fax (213) 436-0750

BRITISH COLUMBIA
MINISTRY OF TOURISM
P.O. Box 9107
Whittier, CA 90608-9107
(310) 696-1985
Fax (310) 696-5615

BRITISH TOURIST
AUTHORITY
350 S. Figueroa St. #450
Los Angeles, CA 90071
(213) 628-5731
Fax (213) 628-8681

BRITISH TOURIST
AUTHORITY
2580 Cumberland Pkwy. #470
Atlanta, GA 30339-3909
(404) 524-5856

BULGARIAN EMBASSY
1621 22nd St. N.W.
Washington, DC 20008
(212) 387-7969

CANADIAN CONSULATE
GENERAL
300 S. Grand Ave. #1000
Los Angeles, CA 90071
(213) 346-2700
Fax (213) 620-8827

CANADIAN CONSULATE
TRADE OFFICE
50 Fremont St. #1825
San Francisco, CA 94105
(415) 543-2550 ext. 24
Fax (415) 512-7671

CAYMAN ISLANDS
TOURIST OFFICE
3440 Wilshire Blvd. #1202
Los Angeles, CA 90010
(213) 738-1968
Fax (213) 738-1829

CENTRAL EUROPEAN URS
AND TRAVEL (CEDOK),
including Czech and Slovakia
10 E. 40th St.
New York, NY 10016
(212) 988-8080

REP. OF CHINA, TAIWAN
TOURISM BUREAU
166 Geary St. #1605
San Francisco, CA 94108
(415) 989-8677
Fax (415) 989-7242

COOK ISLANDS TOURIST
AUTHORITY
6033 W. Century Blvd. #690
Los Angeles, CA 90045
(310) 216-2872
Fax (310) 216-2868

CYPRUS TOURISM
  ORGANIZATION
13 E. 40th St.
New York, NY 10016
(212) 213-9100

DANISH TOURIST BOARD
P.O. Box 2722-18
Huntington Beach, CA 92649
(714) 893-7248
Fax (714) 893-7327

DANISH TOURIST BOARD
655 Third Ave.
New York, NY 10017
(212) 949-2333

EGYPTIAN TOURIST
  AUTHORITY
8383 Wilshire Blvd. #215
Beverly Hills, CA 90211
(213) 653-8815
Fax (213) 653-8961

FIJI VISITORS BUREAU
5777 W. Century Blvd. #220
Los Angeles, CA 90045
(310) 568-1616
Fax (310) 670-2318

FINNISH TOURIST BOARD
23715 W. Malibu Rd.
Box 367
Malibu, CA 90265
(818) 225-8490
Fax (818) 225-8492

FINNISH TOURIST BOARD
655 Third Ave.
New York, NY 10017
(212) 949-2333

FRENCH GOVERNMENT
  NATIONAL TOURIST OFFICE
610 Fifth Ave.
New York, NY 10020
(212) 757-1125

FRENCH GOVERNMENT
  TOURIST OFFICE
9454 Wilshire Blvd. #715
Beverly Hills, CA 90212
(310) 271-2358
Fax (310) 276-2835

GERMAN NATIONAL
  TOURIST OFFICE
11766 Wilshire Blvd. #750
Los Angeles, CA 90025
(310) 575-9799
Fax (310) 575-1565

GERMAN NATIONAL
  TOURIST OFFICE
122 E. 42nd St.
Chanin Bldg., 52nd floor
New York, NY 10168-0072
1-800-637-1171

GREEK NATIONAL
  TOURIST OFFICE
611 W. 6th St. #2198
Los Angeles, CA 90017
(213) 626-6696
Fax (213) 489-9744

GREEK NATIONAL
  TOURIST ORGANIZATION
645 Fifth Ave.
New York, NY 10022
(212) 421-5777

HONG KONG TOURIST
  ASSOCIATION
10940 Wilshire Blvd. #1220
Los Angeles, CA 90024
(310) 208-4582
Fax (310) 208-1869

HONG KONG TOURIST
  ASSOCIATION
(415) 421-4582

HUNGARIAN TRAVEL
  BUREAU (IBUSZ)
1 Parker Plaza #1104
Fort Lee, NJ 07024
(201) 592-8585

ICELAND TOURIST BOARD
655 Third Ave.
New York, NY 10017
(212) 949-2333

GOVERNMENT OF INDIA
  TOURIST OFFICE
3550 Wilshire Blvd. #204
Los Angeles, CA 90010
(213) 380-8855
Fax (213) 380-6111

INDONESIA TOURIST
  PROMOTION OFFICE
3457 Wilshire Blvd. #104
Los Angeles, CA 90010
(213) 387-2078
Fax (213) 380-4876

IRISH TOURIST BOARD
17875 Von Karman #202
Irvine, CA 92714
1-800-223-6470 (714) 251-9229
Fax (714) 251-9432

IRISH TOURIST BOARD
757 Third Ave.
New York, NY 10017
(212) 418-0800

ISRAEL GOVERNMENT
  TOURIST OFFICE
6380 Wilshire Blvd. #1700
Los Angeles, CA 90048
(213) 658-7462
Fax (213) 658-6543

ITALIAN GOVERNMENT
  TOURIST BOARD
12400 Wilshire Blvd. #550
Los Angeles, CA 90025
(310) 820-0098
Fax (310) 820-6357

ITALIAN GOVERNMENT
  TRAVEL OFFICE
630 Fifth Ave.
New York, NY 10111
(212) 245-4822

JAPAN NATIONAL TOURIST
  ORGANIZATION
360 Post St. #601
San Francisco, CA 94108
(415) 989-7140
Fax (415) 398-5461

JAPAN NATIONAL TOURIST
  ORGANIZATION
624 S. Grand Ave. #1611
Los Angeles, CA 90017
(213) 623-1952
Fax (213) 623-6301

KENYA TOURIST OFFICE
9150 Wilshire Blvd. #160
Beverly Hills, CA 90212
(310) 274-6635
Fax (310) 859-7010

KOREA NATIONAL TOURISM
  CORPORATION
3435 Wilshire Blvd. #350
Los Angeles, CA 90010
(213) 382-3435
Fax (213) 480-0483

LUXEMBOURG NATIONAL
  TOURIST OFFICE
801 Second Ave.
New York, NY 10017
(212) 370-9850

MACAU TOURIST
  INFORMATION BUREAU
3133 Lake Hollywood Dr.
P.O. Box 1860
Los Angeles, CA 90078
(213) 851-3402
Fax (213) 851-3684

MALAYSIA TOURISM
  PROMOTION BOARD
818 W. 7th St.
Los Angeles, CA 90017
(213) 689-9702
Fax (213) 689-1530

CONSULATE OF MALTA
249 E. 35th St.
New York, NY 10016
(212) 725-2345

MEXICAN GOVERNMENT
  TOURISM OFFICE
10100 Santa Monica Blvd. #224
Los Angeles, CA 90067
(310) 203-8191
Fax (310) 203-8316

MONACO GOVERNMENT
  TOURIST AND CONVENTION
  BUREAU
845 Third Ave., 19th floor
New York, NY 10022
(212) 759-5227

NETHERLANDS BOARD
  OF TOURISM
9841 Airport Blvd. #103
Los Angeles, CA 90045
(310) 348-9339
Fax (310) 348-9344

NETHERLANDS BOARD
  OF TOURISM
355 Lexington Ave.
New York, NY 10017
(212) 370-7360

NEW ZEALAND TOURISM
  OFFICE
501 Santa Monica Blvd. #300
Santa Monica, CA 90401
(310) 395-7480
Fax (310) 395-5453

NORWEGIAN TOURIST BOARD
655 Third Ave.
New York, NY 10017
(212) 949-2333

PHILIPPINE DEPARTMENT
OF TOURISM
447 Sutter St. #507
San Francisco, CA 94108
(415) 956-4060
Fax (415) 956-2093

PHILIPPINE DEPARTMENT
OF TOURISM
3660 Wilshire Blvd. #216
Los Angeles, CA 90010
(213) 487-4525
Fax (213) 386-4063

POLISH NATIONAL TOURIST
OFFICE (ORBIS)
333 N. Michigan Ave.
Chicago, IL 60601
(312) 236-9013

PORTUGUESE NATIONAL
TOURIST OFFICE
590 Fifth Ave., 4th floor
New York, NY 10036
(212) 354-4403

ROMANIA NATIONAL
TOURIST OFFICE
342 Madison Ave.
New York, NY 10017
(212) 697-6971

SINGAPORE TOURIST
PROMOTION BOARD
8484 Wilshire Blvd. #510
Beverly Hills, CA 90211
(213) 852-1901
Fax (213) 852-0129

SOUTH AFRICAN
TOURISM BOARD
9841 Airport Blvd. #1524
Los Angeles, CA 90045
(310) 641-8444
Fax (310) 641-5812

NATIONAL TOURIST
OFFICE OF SPAIN
1221 Brickell Ave. #1850
Miami, FL 33131
(305) 358-1992

SWISS NATIONAL
TOURIST OFFICE
222 N. Sepulveda Blvd. #1570
El Segundo, CA 90245
(310) 335-5980
Fax (310) 335-5982

SWEDISH TOURIST BOARD
655 Third Ave.
New York, NY 10017
(212) 949-2333

SWISS NATIONAL
TOURIST BOARD
608 Fifth Ave.
New York, NY 10020
(212) 757-5944

TOURIST OFFICE OF SYRIA
26691 Plaza #210
Mission Viejo, CA 92691
(714) 582-2905
Fax (714) 582-3585

TOURIST OFFICE OF SPAIN
8383 Wilshire Blvd. #960
Beverly Hills, CA 90211
(213) 658-7188
(213) 658-1061

TAHITI TOURISM BOARD
300 N. Continental Blvd. #180
El Segundo, CA 90245
(310) 414-8484
Fax (310) 414-8490

TOURISM AUTHORITY
  OF THAILAND
3440 Wilshire Blvd. #1100
Los Angeles, CA 90010
(213) 382-2353
Fax (213) 389-7544

TONGA CONSULATE
  GENERAL
360 Post St. #604
San Francisco, CA 94108
(415) 781-0365
Fax (415) 781-3964

TURKISH CULTURE AND
  INFORMATION OFFICE
821 United Nations Plaza
New York, NY 10017
(212) 687-2194

UNITED STATES VIRGIN
  ISLANDS
3460 Wilshire Blvd. #412
Los Angeles, CA 90010
(213) 739-0138
Fax (213) 739-2005

TRAVEL OFFERS

CALLING ALL SENIORS

Grand Circle, the first company to offer programs to Americans 50 years of age and older, is offering a FREE brochure, "101 Tips for Mature Travelers," and a FREE catalog brochure. Grand Circle specializes in unique experiences for seasonal travelers around the world, by both land and sea, and offers optional programs as well as Learning Series lectures, museum visits, and home stays. **For more information, phone 1-800-221-2610 Monday–Friday 8 A.M.–7 P.M., Saturday 9 A.M.–5 P.M. (eastern standard time).**

CAPITOL TRAVEL

If you're planning a summer vacation, consider enjoying the history and patriotism of a trip to Washington, D.C. You can obtain a FREE visitors package containing maps, tour schedules, and motel or bed-and-breakfast (B&B) information. **Write to Washington, D.C., Convention and Visitors Association, 1212 New York Ave., NW, Suite 600, Washington, DC 20005 or phone (202) 789-7000.**

CONNECTIONS

Crampton's International Airport Transit Guide lists schedules and rates for taxis, car services, trains, buses, car rental agencies, and other connections from airports to nearby cities worldwide. The pocket-size guide costs under $5 and is updated yearly. **For more information, write the publisher, Salk International Travel Premiums, Inc., at P.O. Box 1388, Sunset Beach, CA 90742, or phone (213) 592-3315.**

FAST GETAWAY

In today's fast-paced world, few of us can afford the time to take a month-long trip. But that doesn't mean you still can't get away from it all. Plan a quick, short trip with the help of a newsletter that specializes in 2-, 3-, 4-, and 5-day travel opportunities, bargain hotel packages, getaways, special events, festivals, and more. *Quicktrips* is big on 800 numbers, making further information only a few push-buttons away. Each issue is so up to date that travel agents frequently use this publication as a reference tool. **Get a FREE introductory copy by sending a long, self-addressed, stamped envelope to: *Quicktrips*, Sample Issue Offer, P.O. Box 3308, Crofton, MD 21114.**

FREE TRAVEL TIPS AND ADVICE

The Consumer Information Center is offering low-cost travel booklets, including "Discover America," a directory for domestic vacation information, which tells you where to get free maps, travel guides, and event calendars (50¢); "Lesser-Known Areas of the National Park System," which describes the parks that don't need to be booked three summers in advance ($1.50); "Fly-Rights," which offers help in finding low airfares, handling lost tickets and baggage, and dealing with canceled and overbooked flights ($1.75); and "Foreign Entry Requirements," which provides embassy and consulate names and addresses for people wishing to apply for visas (50¢). **To order, send requests to the Consumer Information Center, P.O. Box 100, Pueblo, CO 81002.**

45 PLUS

If you are over 45 and are planning to travel, you will enjoy *The Golden Traveler.* Published every month, *The Golden Traveler* contains travel tips, destination ideas, and travel education opportunities especially geared toward 45-plus travelers. **To receive a sample issue, send $1 for postage and handling to Golden Companions, P.O. Box 754, Pullman, WA 99163.**

JERUSALEM

The Grand Tour of Israel is designed for people with time for a 22-day, relaxed-pace trip. It includes four nights in Tel Aviv and seven nights in Jerusalem. Special features may include a cruise on the Sea of Galilee and a visit to a kibbutz. All breakfasts and dinners are provided. **For more information, write to the American Jewish Congress, 15 E. 84th St., New York, NY 10028, or call 1-800-221-4694.**

KEEP IT SAFE

Seniors and their families worry about falls and highway accidents, as these are the major causes of injury and death among people over 65. But many of these injuries can be prevented. A few precautions may keep you or someone you care about from becoming a statistic. The Association of Trial Lawyers of America and the Johns Hopkins Injury Prevention Center would like to send you a copy of their FREE brochure, "Keep It Safe: At Home on the Road." The brochure details several things you can do to reduce the risk of injury and lists precautions specific to the kinds of accidents seniors are prone to. **To receive the FREE brochure, send a long, self-addressed, stamped envelope to Keep It Safe, P.O. Box 3717, Washington, DC 20007.**

VIVA LAS VEGAS

Heading to Las Vegas? The 12-page monthly publication, *The Las Vegas Advisor,* is a good bet. It's bursting with up-to-the-moment information for visitors to Las Vegas. You will read about the best Vegas values, accommodation deals, coupon promotions, dining, and so forth. This newsletter is a sure bet to get you into the vacation mood. A sample issue is $3. **Write to: Huntington Press, 5280 S. Valley View, Suite B, Las Vegas, NV 89118.**

MAKE ROOM FOR BIG PAPA

In 1987, Hilton Hotels created the Hilton Senior HHonors program. The program offers lodging and dinner discounts at more than 230 participating Hiltons to travelers over 60. Members receive discounts of up to 50 percent on accommodations, and 20 percent discounts on dinners for two at Hilton hotels throughout the United States. The dining discount applies even if members are not guests of the hotel.

In addition to discounts, Senior HHonors members receive other special benefits. **For more information, phone 1-800-492-3232.**

ORANGE YOU GOING TO VISIT?

Enjoy the beautiful beaches, spectacular sunsets, and gracious hospitality of Florida. **For a FREE Florida Vacation Guide, phone (904) 487-1462.**

OUTDOOR VACATIONS FOR WOMEN OVER 40

Outdoor travel adventures are available for women of all skill levels. Woman traveling alone are welcome. Past events include canoeing and exploring the Everglades; cross-country skiing in Mammoth Lakes, California; whale watching in Baja, California; home visits in New Zealand; rafting the Rio Grande; walking tours in Wales and France; sailing on the Chesapeake Bay; and a New England windjammer cruise. Trips led by expert women guides include instruction, lodging, meals, and ground transportation. **For more information, write to Outdoor Vacations for Women Over 40, P.O. Box 200, Groton, MA 01450, or phone (508) 448-3331.**

R&R STANDS FOR FREE

More than 150 discounts and extra values are offered in the Palm Springs Desert Resorts "R&R Club" brochure, available FREE. **To receive a FREE brochure and vacation planner filled with detailed listings of accommodations, dining,** activities, and events, phone the Palm Springs Desert Resorts Convention and Visitors Bureau at 1-800-41-RELAX (417-3529) or write to the Bureau at 69-930 Highway 111, Suite 201, Rancho Mirage, CA 92270.

RECREATIONAL VEHICLE STATISTICS

According to a study conducted by the University of Michigan:

❏ Recreational vehicle (RV) ownership has increased 50 percent among householders ages 55 and up since 1980.

❏ RV ownership rates rise with age, reaching the highest levels among those ages 55 to 74. Ownership of motor homes, conversion vehicles, travel trailers, and fifth-wheels are highest among RVers ages 55 to 64.

❏ Among those 55 and over, the top benefits of RV ownership are freedom to go where and when you want; going camping; visiting family, friends, and new places; using the vehicle as a vacation home; and traveling in familiar comfort.

❏ Americans over 50 have combined incomes of more than $800 billion, control 51 percent of the nation's discretionary income, and account for 40 percent of consumer demand.

❏ Travelers 45 to 54 average four-night trips, the 55-to-64 group averages five nights, and those 65 and older average six nights. **For more information about RVs, contact the Recreation Vehicle Industry Association, 1896 Preston White Dr., Reston, VA 22090-0999, or phone (703) 620-6003.**

ROCKY MOUNTAIN HIGH

All the excitement of the Rockies comes to life in the vibrant city of Denver, Colorado. The city is a unique blend of Western spirit and modern culture. **For your FREE 160-page guide, write Denver & Colorado Visitors Guide, 225 W. Colfax Ave., Denver, CO 80202-5399, or phone 1-800-645-3446.**

SENIOR SAVING ON TRAVEL

Alaska Wildland Adventures offers discounts on selected "Senior Safari" departures. The company specializes in "soft adventure" for those who don't want to sacrifice comfort while exploring the wilderness. Comfort trips include a coach tour through national parks or whale watching on a yacht. **For more information, write to P.O. Box 389, Girdwood, AK 99587, or call 1-800-334-8730.**

SHALL WE BOARD, MY PET?

"Vacationing with Your Pet!" is a 650-page book listing hotels, motels, inns, ranches, and B&Bs that welcome you and your pet. More than 20,000 pet-friendly lodgings are listed. Locate a lodging in your price range at all popular vacation destinations in the United States and Canada. The new edition includes more than 150 pages of helpful training and travel pet tips, making it "dog-gone" handy on your next trip. **To order phone 1-800-496-2665 or send a check, cash, or money order for $19.95 to Pet Friendly Publications, P.O. Box 8459, Scottsdale, AZ 84252.**

STANDBY TRAVEL

If you can be flexible in your plans, you might want to consider standby travel. It can be one of the cheapest ways to fly. Airhitch has offices in several large cities and does most of its business by mail. After you phone for information, a registration form will be sent to you. Then, you apply for the dates and length of stay you desire (which must be at least five days long), and call for availability on the Wednesday before your desired departure dates. Airhitch's phone system is programmed to dispense all the details of the standby program. **For more information, phone 1-800-372-1234 or (212) 864-2000.** Make sure to have a pen and paper ready when calling.

Access International also books standby flights from New York to points in Europe. It works on a registration/fee basis and publishes a brochure that describes the services. **Phone (212) 333-7280 for more information.**

STAY ANYWHERE FOR $25 A DAY

The Educators Bed and Breakfast Network is a travel club for teachers, school staff, and their friends. Once you pay a one-time $35 fee, you receive a membership directory listing the available places and accommodations. After selecting the places you wish to stay, you are charged a $7 booking fee for each host. **For more information about the Educators Bed and Breakfast Network, write Norm or Hazel Smith at P.O. Box 5279, Eugene, OR 97405, or phone 1-800-377-0301.**

STAY UP FOR CARSON

Step back into the past and save. Stake your claim to dynamite discounts in historic Carson City, Nevada. Save up to a third with a Seniors Strike Silver card. As a Silver Club Member,take advantage of two- or three-night getaways from $66 for two to beautiful Old West Nevada. Also included are great discounts on dining, money-saving deals on gaming, and recreation rebates. **For your Seniors Strike Silver card, a trail map, and reservations, phone 1-800-NEVADA-1.**

SWEET NEWS FOR DIABETIC TRAVELERS

A special issue of *The Diabetic Traveler* offers health, exercise, and planning tips for diabetic seniors who want to travel. You will also receive a FREE credit card–size guide to help you adjust your insulin doses when you cross time zones, in addition to a copy of "Management of Diabetes During Intercontinental Travel." **Send a large, self-addressed, stamped envelope, plus $1 postage and handling, to** *The Diabetic Traveler,* **P.O. Box 8223, Stamford, CT 06905, or phone (203) 327-5832.**

WE'LL ALWAYS HAVE PARIS

Paris Notes is an actual slice of Paris life as seen from the eyes of English-speaking locals. This publication is filled with articles about life in the City of Light. Every issue will instantly transport you to a Left Bank sidewalk cafe as you read about the Paris scene, local discoveries, out-of-the-way encounters, and city surprises. Within its pages you'll find descriptions of small bistros where locals gather, little hotels tucked away on private avenues, farmer's markets, unique galleries, and more. **For *Paris Notes*, send two first class stamps to Paris Notes, P.O. Box 3668, Manhattan Beach, CA 90266.**

DEEP IN THE HEART OF TEXAS

There's so much to do in Texas, from the Alamo to the Texas Rangers baseball team and the Dallas Cowboys football team, you won't be able to sit still. As soon as you arrive, you'll be flying by the seat of your pants. Spin on an ornate carousel or twirl on a dusty dance floor. Go into orbit with astronauts or come down to Earth at a chili cook-off. From big cities to small towns, there's a lot of fun to go around. **For the new 272-page Texas Travel Guide, phone 1-800-8888-TEX.**

TOURS FOR THE DISABLED

Travel can be especially trying for persons with disabilities. Whole Person Tours, an enterprise providing tours for the disabled in Europe and the United States, also publishes *The Itinerary,* a bimonthly magazine for the disabled traveler. The cost is $10 for one year, or $18 for two years. **Write to The Itinerary, P.O. Box 1084, Bayonne, NJ 07002.**

TURN YOUR HOLIDAY INTO A SAGA

One of the largest operators specializing in tours and cruises for seniors is Saga Holidays, which started in Great Britain 45 years ago arranging vacations for working-class families. It has operated in the United States since 1980.

The *Saga Holidays Travel Planner* catalog details trips to destinations worldwide. With each trip, Saga offers the following:

❏ Guaranteed prices

❏ Professional tour director

❏ No-penalty cancellation policy; you may cancel for any reason up to 30 days before you travel; in the event of illness, you may cancel up to the day of travel

❏ Medical insurance

❏ Flight and baggage insurance

❏ Reduced admission charges to museums, castles, and attractions on scheduled excursions

❏ Hotel taxes

For catalogs on land tours and cruises, call Saga Holidays at 1-800-343-0273.

WHERE TO PARK YOUR RV

More than ever before, people are opting to see the country in an RV. There are more than 16,000 publicly and privately owned RV campgrounds nationwide, providing campers with stops throughout the country. Some RV parks feature golf courses, tennis courts, swimming pools, and fitness centers. Would-be RVers are advised to rent different models before buying. RVs range in price and style from spartan to luxurious and costly. Different types of RVs include truck campers, travel trailers, folding camping trailers, and motor homes.

Consult these useful guides for information on renting RVs, selecting campgrounds, preparing and packing for your trip, driving tips, setting up your camp, and more: *Camping Vacation Planner* (**FREE by calling 1-800-47-SUNNY**); *Set Free in an RV* (**send $3 postage and handling to RVIA Publications Dept. SS, P.O. Box 2999, Reston, VA 22090**); **and** *Who's Who in RV Rentals* (**send $7.50 postage and handling to the Recreation Vehicle Rental Association, 3930 University Dr., Fairfax, VA 22030**).

TRAVEL NEWSLETTERS

Travel Smart

FOR A FREE SAMPLE ISSUE, WRITE TO:

Travel Smart
Dobbs Ferry, NY 10522

PHONE:
1-800-327-3633

Travel Smart is a monthly, 12-page newsletter featuring 3 pages devoted to travel deals, plus other, more general articles.

Consumer Reports Travel Letter

FOR A FREE SAMPLE ISSUE, WRITE TO:

Consumer Reports Travel Letter Subscription Dept. P.O. Box 51366 Boulder, CO 80321-1366

PHONE:
Delta Publishing
1-800-728-3728

Consumer Reports Travel Letter is a monthly publication containing many of the same types of charts and comparisons you'll find in *Consumer Reports.*

TravLtips

FOR A FREE SAMPLE ISSUE, WRITE TO:

TravLtips
163-07 Depot Rd.
P.O. Box 580188
Flushing, NY 11358

PHONE:
(718) 939-2400

TravLtips is for people who like to spend time on the ocean but not at cruise prices. The bi-monthly magazine focuses on freighter travel. The newsletter includes answers to the most commonly asked questions concerning freighter travel as well as several innovative ways to cut the costs of sea travel while extending your time afloat.

Budget Travel

FOR A FREE SAMPLE ISSUE, WRITE TO:

Budget Travel
Arthur Frommer, Inc.
1841 Broadway
New York, NY 10023

Budget Travel is put together by Arthur Frommer, author of the "Dollar-A-Day" series of books. From his varied experiences, Frommer recommends inexpensive vacations offered by travel agencies and tour operators that he has personally worked with in the past.

Best Fares

FOR A FREE SAMPLE ISSUE,
WRITE TO:

**Best Fares
P.O. Box 171212
Arlington, TX 76003**

PHONE:

1-800-576-1234

Best Fares is considered by many frequent fliers to be the authority on getting the lowest airfares. It is a must for the man or woman on the go.

Travel Companions

FOR MORE INFORMATION,
WRITE TO:

**Travel Companions
Box 833
Amityville, NY
11701-0833**

PHONE:

**1-800-392-1258
or (516) 454-0880
fax (516) 454-0170**

Travel Companions is full of news on travel discounts, along with tips and encouragement for lone travelers, consumer advice, and scores of personal ads from singles seeking travel companions (most list their first name, age, height, weight, and interests). Six issues yearly. A typical issue contains 18–20 pages of editorial content and about another 28 pages of personal ads. A one-year subscription costs $48 (including six back issues), with up to six personal ads for $159.

Susie's Travel Bug News

FOR A FREE SAMPLE ISSUE,
WRITE TO:
Susie's Travel Bug News
1660 S. Albion St.
Suite 309
Denver, CO 80222

PHONE:
1-800-592-TRVL

Susie's Travel Bug News bills itself as "your time-saving guide to great destinations, exciting adventures, quick tips, and value-packed bargains."

Passport Newsletter

FOR MORE INFORMATION,
WRITE TO:
Passport Newsletter
350 W. Hubbard St.
Suite 440
Chicago, IL 60610

PHONE:
1-800-542-6670.

Passport Newsletter concentrates on destinations, hotels, restaurants, and shopping. Twelve issues yearly. A typical issue consists of 20–24 pages. A one-year subscription costs $75.

The Shipboard Cruiser

FOR MORE INFORMATION,
WRITE TO:
The Shipboard Cruiser
P.O. Box 533737
Orlando, FL 32853-3737

PHONE:
(407) 422-6095

The Shipboard Cruiser contains information on cruise ships. A typical issue is about 12 pages and comes out monthly. A one-year subscription costs $49.

Island Escapes

FOR MORE INFORMATION, WRITE TO:

**Island Escapes
3886 State St.
Santa Barbara, CA 93105**

PHONE:
1-800-477-3575

Island Escapes concentrates on service information and focuses on one island per month. September featured Italy's Ponza, "an overlooked pearl" that reminds many of Capri 50 years ago. Twelve issues yearly; a typical issue is about 8 pages. A one-year subscription is $39.

The Italian Traveler

FOR MORE INFORMATION, WRITE TO:

**The Italian Traveler
P.O. Box 32
Livingston, NJ 07039**

PHONE:
**1-800-362-6978
or (201) 535-6572**

The Italian Traveler reviews restaurants and lodgings throughout Italy. Eleven issues come out yearly. A one-year susbscription is $59.

Las Vegas Advisor

FOR MORE INFORMATION, WRITE TO:

**Las Vegas Advisor
5280 S. Valley View,
Suite B
Las Vegas, NV 89118**

PHONE:
1-800-244-2224

Las Vegas Advisor analyzes Vegas casinos and other attractions from the consumer's point of view. A recent issue explained the management changes at the MGM Grand Hotel, listed upcoming performers, and offered a list of 10 top values in town, from room rates to buffets. A one-year subscription of 12 issues is $45.

The Way to Go

SEND:
**A long SASE with two
first class stamps affixed**

ASK FOR:
**"A Consumer's Guide
to Renting a Car"**

MAIL TO:
**Alamo Rent A Car
P.O. Box 13005
Atlanta, GA 30324**

If you've ever been confused over the endless number of options available when choosing a rent-a-car, "A Consumer's Guide to Renting a Car," FREE from Alamo Rent-A-Car, can help. It's a handy glovebox-size booklet that helps you be a smart consumer. It even includes a comparison worksheet that allows you to determine which rental company offers you the best deal.

Pack Your Bags

SEND:
**A long SASE with two
first class stamps affixed**

ASK FOR:
**Sample copy of
*The Thrifty Traveler***

MAIL TO:
**The Thrifty Traveler
P.O. Box 8168-F
Clearwater, FL 34618**

Never pay full price for travel. *The Thrifty Traveler* monthly newsletter will show you how to stretch your travel dollar, whether you're traveling around the country or around the world. Each issue is jam-packed with news, tips, resources, and special deals.

A FREE sample issue of *The Thrifty Traveler* (normally $2.50) is available ONLY to FREEBIES readers. You'll also receive a special subscription offer.

Best Western Where Guide

PHONE:
1-800-528-1234

ASK FOR:
**1996 Best Western Road
Atlas and Travelers'
Guide**

"The 1996 Best Western Road Atlas and Travelers' Guide" provides information and maps for more than 2,000 Best Western hotels in the United States, Canada, Mexico, the Caribbean, and Central America. Besides hotel information, this FREE 292-page guide lists many points of interest. Also included with the guide is an eight panel foldout pamphlet, "Traveler Safety Tips."

Travel Tips

If one good tip deserves another, then you'll get plenty within each issue of *Travel Smart*. There are more than 100 travel tips in every issue! This is a publication for the world traveler looking to travel better for less. Read all about discount airfare opportunities, package deals, and special bargains not found elsewhere. You'll discover interesting articles covering vacation destinations and retreats, senior travel suggestions, and more.

Travelin' Talk

Travelin' Talk is an international "network" dedicated to providing assistance to travelers with disabilities. You'll receive a quarterly newsletter that covers new resources, membership updates, and travel experiences and encounters, and features stories on how members are helping others as a part of the organization. The newsletter is FREE with membership and dues are based on a sliding scale.

Europe Through the Back Door

SEND:

On a plain piece of paper write, "Send me your latest newsletter/catalog via first class" and enclose three first class stamps

ASK FOR:

Europe Through the Back Door

MAIL TO:

**Europe Through the Back Door
120 4th Ave. N.
P.O. Box 2009
Edmonds, WA
98020-2009**

Here is a *FREE* 64-page newsletter/catalog which, regardless of your age or budget, helps you explore Europe with confidence as a temporary local. Each quarterly issue is filled with articles and "road scholar" letters. A recent edition covers offbeat Britain, untouristy Greece, and the latest train travel opportunities throughout Europe.

Safety First

SEND:
A SASE

ASK FOR:
A FREE copy of
Traveler Safety Tips

MAIL TO:

**The American Hotel and Motel Association
1201 New York Ave. NW
Suite 600
Washington, DC 20005**

The American Hotel and Motel Association offers a free guide for traveler safety tips.

Lookie Here! It's Art Bell!

SEND:
**$4 for a back issue,
$29.95 for one year
(12 issues)**

ASK FOR:
**Art Bell's
*After Dark Newsletter***

MAIL TO:
**Art Bell's After Dark
Newsletter
744 E. Pine St.
Central Point, OR 97502**

Art Bell's national radio program, "After Dark," is heard by over 5 million listeners on weekday evenings. Topics of discussion cover UFO landings, crop circles, earthquake predictions, and even dead chicken revivals. Art Bell's *After Dark Newsletter* goes one step beyond the radio show by putting into print more of the same topics discussed on the air. The addition of color photographs now gives this monthly newsletter even more appeal.

GENERAL OFFERS

You've heard the expression "Save the best for last." With that in mind, we invite you to peruse the General Offers Section. Inside you'll find a variety of FREE and almost-FREE offers collected to aid you in the different aspects of your daily life, from health, beauty, and personal safety, to things for the grandkids and more. Our editors have reviewed literally hundreds of offers before making the selections for this book. Each offer is described as accurately as possible.

HOW TO ENSURE THAT YOU GET WHAT YOU ASK FOR

1. **Follow the directions.** Each offer specifies how to order the freebie. Some offers may ask for a long, self-addressed, stamped envelope (SASE). Be sure to check

the amount of postage requested. Some offers may require two first class stamps. Likewise, offers from Canada will require the correct postage amount. Since postal rates have changed, check with your local post office to determine the correct first class postage to Canada. If a small postage and handling (P&H) fee is requested, include the proper amount (a check or money order is usually preferred). Some suppliers may wait for out-of-town checks to clear before honoring requests. If you are sending coins, use a single piece of tape to fasten them down.

2. **Print all information.** Not everyone's handwriting is easy to read. Neatly print your name, address, and the complete spelling of your city and state on your request. Be sure to include your return address on the outside of your mailing envelope. Use a ballpoint pen when you write, because pencils can often smear, and felt-tip or ink pens easily smudge.

3. **Allow time for your request to be processed and sent.** Some suppliers send their offers by first class mail. Others use bulk-rate mail, which can take up to eight weeks. Suppliers get thousands of requests each year and may process them slowly or right away, depending on the time of year.

AUTOMOTIVE

Body Talk

SEND:
A long SASE

ASK FOR:
"How to Choose the Right Body Shop"

MAIL TO:
**ASE Body Shop Brochure
Dept. FR-B96
P.O. Box 347
Herndon, VA 22070**

As a car owner, your chances of needing the services of a collision repair and refinishing facility are greater than you think. It's important to know how to select a body shop and what questions to ask once you've selected one. The National Institute for Automotive Service Excellence wants to help you make that tough decision with their **FREE brochure, "How to Choose the Right Body Shop."**

The Easy Way to Clean Everything

SEND:
$1 P&H

ASK FOR:
Protect All "Duopak"

MAIL TO:
**Protect All, Inc.
P.O. Box 5968
Orange, CA 92613-5968**

Is there an easy way to clean everything? Yes! Send for a **trial package of Protect All "Duopak,®"** which contains samples of the "Quick & Easy Wash" and "Polish, Wax & Treatment" formulas. "Quick & Easy Wash" allows you to wash an entire vehicle without a hose or rinsing.

Protect All "Polish, Wax & Treatment" cleans, polishes, and treats all surfaces—front to back, inside and out. It leaves an anti-static, water-repellent, lustrous shine on hard surfaces while protecting vinyl, rubber, and plastic. Great for vehicles and hundreds of home and office applications, it works on fiberglass, aluminum, wood, paint, glass—in short, it does it all.

Heart Like a Wheel

PHONE:
**1-800-9-FIRESTONE
(1-800-9-934-7378)**

ASK FOR:
Car Care Tips Brochure

A **FREE** 15-page car care **informational brochure from Firestone Tires** has finally been published in plain and easy-to-understand English. Every nonmechanic ought to appreciate this "mini-course" on how to better understand your car's operation.

Professional auto racer (and certified mechanic) Pat Lazzaro has put together plenty of helpful information in this publication. There is even a handy car maintenance chart included. Best of all, it is available **FREE** of charge by calling a toll-free telephone number.

Summer Break

SEND:
A long SASE

ASK FOR:
"Getting Your Vehicle Ready for Summer"

MAIL TO:
**ASE Summer Brochure
Dept. FR-S96
P.O. Box 347
Herndon, VA 22070**

Get you car ready for summer's heat, dust, and stop-and-go traffic with the National Institute for Automotive Service Excellence's **FREE brochure, "Getting Your Vehicle Ready for Summer."** From your air-conditioning and cooling systems to your brakes and tires, the brochure addresses many of the problem areas that can lead to mechanical failure and suggests easy ways to prevent them.

COLLECTIBLES AND MEMORABILIA

Add to Your Collection

SEND:
Your name and address

ASK FOR:
Linn's Stamp Collecting Made Easy

MAIL TO:
**Linn's Stamp News
P.O. Box 29
Sidney, OH 45365**

Stamp collecting is one of the world's most popular hobbies. Some stamps can increase in value over the years if you know how to preserve and display them properly. The best way to learn is to send for your **FREE copy of *Linn's Stamp Collecting Made Easy,*** a 94-page booklet filled with facts and instructions for the novice or the experienced collector. Complete with information, definitions of terms, and detailed illustrations, this guide is a perfect introduction to stamp collecting.

Back to Nature

If you want to get into the ever-popular hobby of stamp collecting, this assortment of **100 foreign nature design stamps** is a natural selection to start with.

154

SEND:
$2 P&H

ASK FOR:
Nature Stamps

MAIL TO:
**Nature Stamps
P.O. Box 466
Port Washington, NY
11050**

Each stamp depicts a different aspect of nature, including illustrations of birds, animals, flowers, and other natural wonders of the earth.

Each is a real foreign postage stamp in near-mint condition— even the cancellation marks are almost unnoticeable.

Boys of Summer

SEND:
$2 P&H

ASK FOR:
Official Government Baseball Stamps

MAIL TO:
**Consumers Technology Baseball Stamps
P.O. Box 3320
Milford, CT 06460**

A sure catch for any baseball fan or stamp collector, each of these **eight official international postage stamps** of baseball's greatest players bears a colorful action photo of a player along with his team's official logo. You might receive Cal Ripken, Babe Ruth, Mickey Mantle, Don Mattingly, Nolan Ryan, Roger Clemens, Roberto Clemente, or many more. It includes free directions on how to start your own collection and get a free album! All stamps are licensed by both major league baseball and the players association.

Collector's Guidelines

SEND:
A long SASE

ASK FOR:
Sample copy of
Collector's Guidelines
newsletter.

MAIL TO:
Collector's Guidelines
1390 Carling Dr.
Suite 108
St. Paul, MN 55108

If you are an avid collector and want information about news, notes, and inside secrets for collecting, then a **FREE copy of** ***Collector's Guidelines*** may be just the publication for you. *Collector's Guidelines* is a monthly newsletter about collectibles. Along with various articles about numerous collections and hobbies, *Collector's Guidelines* contains sections with questions and answers and advertisements that may help you find the collector's items you've been looking for. To receive your FREE copy of the newsletter, send away today.

Elvis Express

SEND:
Your name and address

ASK FOR:
A FREE sample copy or
subscription information

MAIL TO:
Graceland Express
P.O. Box 16508
Memphis, TN 38180

The universal appeal of Elvis Presley is as legendary as "the King" himself. Old fan? New fan? You'll appreciate this publication. Cost is $12 per year and new subscriptions start with the current issue. Each edition averages 16 pages and is a collectible in itself, with many rare photographs from the Graceland archives.

Golden Days of Radio

SEND:
Your name and address plus $2 P&H

ASK FOR:
A sample issue of *RadioGram* and membership information

MAIL TO:
**SPERDVAC
RadioGram Sample and Information
P.O. Box 7177
Van Nuys, CA 91409**

If you enjoy catching a replay of an old-time radio show such as "Jack Benny," "Amos and Andy," or "The Shadow," then you must get a copy of *RadioGram*. It's filled with news about early radio broadcasting, performers from the Golden Age of Radio, and the preservation of radio comedy and variety shows. Based in Southern California, membership is 1,700 strong and many members are Hollywood old-timers who share their experiences and stories about the heyday of radio.

"O" Pin Season

SEND:
$2 P&H (for each pin)

ASK FOR:
Barcelona Olympics Pin

MAIL TO:
**Pins by Mail
P.O. Box 41630
Tucson, AZ 85717**

Atlanta 1996—site of the 24th Summer Olympics hosted by the United States. However, the most popular event won't take place on the field. That's because the most exciting activity is the trading of commemorative pins. To introduce you to pin collecting, Bill Nelson, the foremost collector in the country and a retired teacher, is offering you **a pin**

from the 1992 Barcelona Games. The pin you will receive is exactly like the ones given to athletes and volunteers at the games and features the Barcelona logo. You'll also receive a FREE issue of the *Bill Nelson Newsletter,* a publication that covers pin collecting.

Presidential Address

SEND:
Your name and address

ASK FOR:
White House Photo Tour Book

MAIL TO:
The White House Washington, DC 20500

Even if your vacation plans did not include a trip to Washington, D.C., you can still visit through this FREE book. Let the White House come to you with the **FREE White House Photo Tour Book.** This 32-page, glossy, full-color book takes you on a tour through every room in the White House, from the Oval Office to the Rose Garden. No room is off limits to you with this book. (Please allow at least 12 weeks for delivery.)

Presidential Salute

SEND:
The person's name and address at least eight to ten weeks in advance of the birthday or anniversary

ASK FOR:
Birthday or Anniversary Card

MAIL TO:
**The President
c/o Greeting Office
The White House
Washington, DC 20500**

Surprise an older friend or relative with a card from the president of the United States! If someone you know is at least 80 years old or has been married for at least 50 years, you can ask the White House to send them a special **FREE Presidential Greeting Card** to help celebrate the occasion. (Please send your request at least 12 weeks in advance.)

Stamps, Stamps, and More Stamps

SEND:
$2 P&H

ASK FOR:
5 Plate Block Stamps

MAIL TO:
**J. Alexander
P.O. Box 7
Roslyn, NY 11576**

Attention all budding or long-time stamp collectors! You can either expand your collection or begin one. This offer includes **five different Full-Gum Mint U.S. 3-cent Plate Blocks.** Stamps vary from authentic Red Cross stamps to stamps displaying past presidents.

State Attractions

SEND:
$1 P&H

ASK FOR:
**State Magnet;
specify state**

MAIL TO:
**Special Products
Dept. T
P.O. Box 6605
Del Ray Beach, FL
33482-6605**

No matter where you hail from, you'll be in the state of happiness when you get your very own **state magnet.** Get a colorful rubberized magnet in the exact shape of your favorite of the 50. Order any state you want, whether it be the state you live in or the state of your favorite sports team.

Your Own Collection

SEND:
$1 P&H

ASK FOR:
A sample copy of
Collecting **magazine**

MAIL TO:
**Odyssey Publications
510 #A So. Corona Mall
Corona, CA 91719-1420**

Finally, a publication that specializes in a variety of the most popular and rarest collectibles. The collectibles include entertainment props, costumes, memorabilia, rare movie posters, original animation cels, one-of-a-kind sports collectibles, and other items owned, used, or signed by famous personalities from various periods of history. *Collecting* **magazine** intends to fulfill your appetite for the fascinating field of collecting.

CONSUMER AWARENESS

A Full Refund

SEND:
Two loose first class postage stamps and your name and address (on an address label if possible)

ASK FOR:
Sample copy of
Refund World
(Limit 1 per address)

MAIL TO:
Refund World
Box 16001
Philadelphia, PA 19114

Refund World is a monthly bulletin that combines the latest refund offers with important information about consumer products, including recall notices and new product releases.

Send for a **FREE sample issue of** *Refund World,* and you'll be on the pipeline to receive hundreds of offers from all over the country—many of which are only advertised locally, but are valid nationally. Complete details are provided for obtaining each refund.

Taken at the Cleaners

CALL:
The NCA at
(212) 967-3002 for the office nearest you.

Usually your dry cleaner removes spots. But what should you do if your expensive garment comes back with a new stain and the cleaner says it's not their fault? The Neighborhood Cleaners Association (NCA) can help.

Send the garment to the NCA and they will analyze the spot and determine if your cleaner was at fault. If the cleaner is at fault, the NCA will send you a claim form to submit to them. The NCA will help mediate any unresolved problems relating to the replacement cost of the garment.

CRAFTS AND HOBBIES

Bringing You Reading with a Passion

SEND:
$2 P&H

ASK FOR:
Sample copy of
Romance Times Magazine

MAIL TO:
Romance Times
Magazine
55 Berger St.
Brooklyn, NY 11211

Are you constantly looking for a novel to sweep you away from your everyday life? Well, look no further. *Romance Times Magazine,* published monthly, is the bible for the romance novel industry. The magazine includes reviews of 150 new romance novels each month, has a column about the comings and goings of celebrities, interviews the most popular

authors, and gives readers an in-depth description of their lives, tastes, and writing styles. Send away for your sample issue and learn about the hottest new romance novels.

Crafty Card

SEND:
$1 P&H

ASK FOR:
**Cross-Stitch
Greeting Card**

MAIL TO:
**Village Crafts FBCS
17000 Tideview Dr.
Anchorage, AK 99511**

This fun **cross-stitch greeting card kit** includes aida cloth, a card with die-cut opening, envelope, and embroidery cotton for one card, plus illustrated instructions for five different designs: rose, dove, heart, cats, or birthday elephants. Look them over and make the one that you like the best. You can create a card for your best friend, your mom, or anyone else special to you.

Crocheting Forever

SEND:
A long SASE

ASK FOR:
Free Crochet Patterns

MAIL TO:
Crocheting Forever
Mary Barbee
11511 Pucker St.
Niles, MI 49120-9036

Do you enjoy crocheting, or would you like to learn how to crochet? You can send away for **two FREE patterns for crocheted doilies.** They will look pretty on your dresser, or you can make them as gifts for Mom or Grandma. They are also quick and easy to make.

Get Together

SEND:
A long SASE

ASK FOR:
"Get-Together Ideas from Cracker Barrel Cheese"

MAIL TO:
Get-Together Ideas from Cracker Barrel Cheese
P.O. Box 490513
El Paso, TX 88549-0513

Every day is filled with memorable moments and tiny triumphs that give us a reason to celebrate. Sometimes it's as simple as exploring a box of old photos you just found in the attic or sitting down to celebrate the completion of a big project. Stopping to savor these moments with family and friends can turn into a special afternoon or evening. Cracker Barrel Cheese would like to assist you with these special moments and other occasions that may call for entertaining or celebrating.

Send away for their **FREE booklet, "Get-Together Ideas from Cracker Barrel Cheese"** and you won't be caught off guard the next time you have company.

Notable Art

SEND:
$1.50 P&H

ASK FOR:
4 Art Print Notecards

MAIL TO:
**Women's Economic Ventures
1387 Schoolhouse Rd.
Santa Barbara, CA 93108**

Embellished stationery is always a nice way to keep in touch with a friend. But these **art print notecards** will give your greetings a special-delivery touch. Each card features a beautiful print created by talented artists from Santa Barbara, California.

Printed on smooth, white cardstock, each card showcases colorful art on the front in a variety of themes and styles. The artist's name and a short biography appear on the back, and the inside is left blank for your personal note. You will receive four notecards and envelopes with each order.

Quilty as Charged

As generations of American families will attest, a well-made quilt is a priceless heirloom. Send for a **package of quilt patterns** and make your own hand-crafted treasures.

Choose from three separate projects: "Afternoon Tea" contains patterns for assembling a set of table dressings, "Classic Cornice Quilts" shows you how to make curtains with two coordinating valances, and "Appliquéed Floor Quilts" provides directions for making three decorative floor throws.

Each project includes a list of materials needed, full-size patterns, and a color picture of the finished work.

Pretty Postage

Want to send a letter that will really grab someone's attention? Then you'll love these **four FREE brightly colored and/or decorated postals.** They measure 5 ½" by 9" and are easily

SEND:
Your name and address

ASK FOR:
Postals

MAIL TO:
Woolie Works
6201 E. Huffman Rd.
Anchorage, AK 99516

assembled. Just fold the sturdy paper, attach the matching sticker, and they're ready for mailing (stamps not included). They're great for those quick little notes or that thank-you you've been meaning to send.

Small Sprouts

SEND:
$1 P&H

ASK FOR:
Window Greenhouse

MAIL TO:
Kids
Dept. F
P.O. Box 3498
San Rafael, CA 94912

Gardening is fascinating, especially when you see the results of your hard work. With the **Window Greenhouse,** you'll have fun while learning about nature at the same time.

This specially designed poly bag makes seed germination and plant growth easy. All you have to do is add about two inches of soil to the bag, sprinkle in the provided seed mixture, water it, and place it in a sunny window. In just a few days, small sprouts will begin to appear and so will a smile on your face.

Something for Nothing

SEND:

$2 P&H for a sample issue or $4.95 for a one-year, five-issue subscription (regular subscription rate is $8.95)

ASK FOR:

Sample issue of *Freebies* or a One-Year Subscription (as indicated above)

MAIL TO:

Freebies/Seniors Offer
1135 Eugenia Pl.
P.O. Box 5025
Carpinteria, CA 93014

Can you use fun items such as ruler stickers, fun pencils, novelty erasers, holiday craft projects, and more? Can you use educational items and informative publications? Then you need *Freebies* **Magazine.** Each issue features approximately 100 useful, informative, and fun items that are available for free or for a small postage-and-handling charge.

Stencil Me In

SEND:

$1 P&H

ASK FOR:

Custom Stencil; specify name up to 10 spaces long

MAIL TO:

Great Tracers
Dept. ST
3 N. Shoenbeck Rd.
Prospect Heights, IL 60070

Make your mark in the world with your own **custom-cut stencil.** Just give Great Tracers any name or word (up to 10 spaces) and they will craft a stencil with $5/8''$ tall letters on durable oil board. The stencil is useful for many craft applications and comes with an idea sheet that lists other fun ways to use it.

Trekker Treat

When the words "To boldly go where no man has gone before" opened the first "Star Trek" television broadcast, no one could have imagined how far the *Enterprise* would eventually travel.

If you're one of the millions of Trek fans, get yourself a **Star Trek window decal** for your own treks. There are two different designs; one says "Starfleet Academy" and the other, "Vulcan Science Academy." Order one and the supplier will select a design for you, or order two and you'll receive one of each.

Water Wise

To help conserve water, DIG Corporation has created a **FREE booklet entitled "Wise Watering for Beautiful Gardens."** Filled with color photos and informative illustrations, this easy-to-read booklet contains useful gardening suggestions for creating and maintaining a water-wise, efficient landscape. Also included are $4 worth of rebate coupons for DIG drip watering kits.

FOOD AND COOKING

Bayou for You

SEND:
$1 P&H

ASK FOR:
**3 Packets of
Magic Seasonings
(Limit 1 request per
address)**

MAIL TO:
**Magic Seasoning Blends
P.O. Box 23342
Dept. MS
New Orleans, LA 70183**

Straight from Chef Paul Prudhomme's K-Paul's Louisiana Kitchen are some great new seasonings that are both delicious and healthy for you! Send for **three sample packets of Chef Paul Prudhomme's Poultry Magic, Vegetable Magic, and Hot & Sweet Pizza & Pasta Magic seasoning blends.**

You'll also receive a catalog packed with dozens of fabulous Cajun food items, eight Chef Paul recipes, and a $5 coupon toward any purchase over $25.

Better with Buttermilk

PHONE:
1-800-373-7226

ASK FOR:
**Low-fat Recipes and
Saco Buttermilk Sample
(Limit 1 per address)**

A touch of buttermilk can make anything you bake better. You'll find all the goodness of real churned buttermilk in Saco's Cultured Buttermilk Blend. Try a **FREE 1-ounce sample of Saco**

Buttermilk Blend, the convenient, contemporary way to bring back that country-fresh, old-fashioned flavor.

You'll also receive a set of 11 low-fat recipes, helpful hints for a healthier diet, and money-saving coupons on other Saco products available at your local grocer.

Bite-Size Delight

SEND:
$1 P&H

ASK FOR:
**Sample of Aplets
& Cotlets**

MAIL TO:
**Aplets & Cotlets
P.O. Box 202
Dept. XA
Cashmere, WA 98815**

For a delightful change of pace from processed sugar and chocolate candies, try a 1.75-ounce sample pack direct from Washington State. Made with pure apple and apricot purees, crunchy walnuts, natural flavors, and no preservatives, these confections are slow-cooked using a country family recipe. You'll also receive a money-saving coupon.

The Catfish Are Jumping!

SEND:
Your name and address

ASK FOR:
Free Brochure

MAIL TO:
Catfish:
The Cultured Fish
P.O. Box 562
Gibbstown, NJ 08027

The catfish are jumping—genuine U.S. farm-raised catfish, that is. **The Catfish Institute's FREE brochure** takes a look at the farm-raised catfish industry. This full-color brochure gives readers the inside story on catfish farming and the production process and explains how this traditional Southern delicacy is now the number one farmed finfish and the fifth most popular fish in America. In addition, simple, tantalizing catfish recipes are featured, as well as consumer tips for selecting the freshest and safest seafood. Send away for your FREE copy.

A Free Taste

Tired of trying to think up new ways to prepare the same old meals? Send for **Gloria Pitzer's FREE flyer with 15 sample Secret Recipes.** "The Recipe Detective," as Pitzer is commonly known, has been re-creating the most popular secret recipes at

SEND:
A long SASE

ASK FOR:
15 Sample Secret Recipes

MAIL TO:
**Gloria Pitzer's
Secret Recipes
P.O. Box 237
Marysville, MI 48040**

home for the past 20 years. Some of her most requested facsimiles are known as Reese's Peanut Butter Cups, Famous Nameless Chocolate Chip Cookies, Big Bucket in the Sky Fried Chicken, and Lone John Silver Fish and Chips. Send away for your FREE 15 Sample Secret Recipes today and you'll also receive information on ordering the "Secret Recipe" newsletter and cookbook.

Great Balls of Fun

SEND:
**$1 P&H for one
or $1.75 for two**

ASK FOR:
Popcorn Ball Maker

MAIL TO:
**Jolly Time Popcorn
P.O. Box 178FBB
Sioux City, IA 51102**

Making homemade snacks has never been so much fun! The makers of Jolly Time popcorn offer the **Jolly Time popcorn ball maker,** the essential tool for turning out honey or caramel popcorn balls. The ball makers come with recipes and complete instructions. Get one and have a ball!

Home Canners Catalog

SEND:
Your name and address

ASK FOR:
Home Canners Catalog

MAIL TO:
**Alltrista Corp.
Dept. FB
P.O. Box 2005
Muncie, IN 47307-0005**

Alltrista's Home Canners Catalog is a collection of products for all of you who create lifelong memories in your kitchen. For flavor, nutrition, and personal reward, nothing equals the rich tradition of home cooking and preserving. The marketers of Ball Home Canning Products have understood that for years. Send away for your **FREE home canner catalog** and browse through the pages of specialty items. As a standard, the company stands behind everything it offers, guaranteeing your satisfaction.

No Yolks!

SEND:
$1 for one, $2 for both

ASK FOR:
**Egg Yolk Separator
and/or Four-in-One
Measuring Spoon**

MAIL TO:
**Pineapple Appeal
538 Maple Dr.
P.O. Box 197
Owatonna, MN 55060**

Did you know that using two egg whites is equivalent to using one whole egg when cooking or baking? Substituting extra egg whites for the yolk is a great way to cut down on fat and cholesterol. With this offer you'll receive **a plastic egg yolk separator** that quickly and easily separates the whites from the yolk. You can also get a **four-in-one measuring spoon,** which has a tablespoon, teaspoon, $1/2$- and $1/4$-teaspoon sizes all in one spoon. The spoon reads ADD FLA-VOR NOT FAT to remind you that seasoning can make low-fat meals taste great.

Pizzas, Tacos, Burgers, and More

SEND:
$4 P&H and a self-addressed label

ASK FOR:
Not Just a Salad **Book**

MAIL TO:
Cheryl Sindell, Nutritionist P.O. Box 49-1955 Los Angeles, CA 90049

"You can eat delicious dishes in any restaurant and still lose weight," says Cheryl Sindell, nutritionist and author of *Not Just a Salad: How to Eat Well and Stay Healthy When Dining Out.*

This is the definitive guide on how to make smart menu selections when dining out. It offers hundreds of recommendations for ordering American, Italian, Chinese, Mexican, and other ethnic cuisines. It even offers strategies for fast-food and airline meals. The foreword of this book was written by world-renowned chef Wolfgang Puck.

Not Just a Salad has been praised by media and medical professionals. This 288-page book sells for $12.95 in stores nationally. But, by special arrangement with the author, you can have this book delivered direct to you for only $4.50. Cheryl Sindell will also autograph copies on request.

175

HEALTH AND BEAUTY

Beautiful Baldness

SEND:
A long SASE

ASK FOR:
The Chrome Dome

MAIL TO:
**Bald Headed Men
of America
102 Bald Dr.
Morehead, NC 28557**

The Bald Headed Men of America issues a newsletter "every now and then" to its 20,000-plus members expounding the good-hearted nature and benefits of being bald in America. The newsletter is aptly titled **"The Chrome Dome."** Men from every walk of life attend the group's annual conventions and participate in a wealth of activities which even include a "Bald as a Golf Ball Golf Tournament."

The organization even has its own line of "Bald Is Beautiful" merchandise, including a toothless comb.

Go Back in Time

Want to look younger? Use this 5-ounce, 15-day **sample of Retinol A** twice daily and see astounding results within a

SEND:

$1 P&H

ASK FOR:

**Retinol A Sample
(Limit 1 per address)**

MAIL TO:

**21st Century Cosmetics
Dept. RA124
10 Chestnut St.
Spring Valley, NY 10977**

short time. Retinol A nourishes and protects your skin while combating the visual signs of aging. What are you waiting for? Order today and turn back the years.

A Hair Workout

SEND:

$2 P&H

ASK FOR:

Sample of Intensive Treatment

MAIL TO:

**Jingles International
115 Albany Post Rd.
Buchanan, NY 10511**

Jingles International has come up with the solution to the limp, lifeless hair dilemma. Hydro Kinetic® Intensive Treatment is a rich formula of herbal extracts, organic moisturizers, natural oils, and essential proteins to revitalize, strengthen, and revive your hair. It is excellent for permed or colored hair. It contains no artificial colors, is not tested on animals, and can be obtained only through professional salons. You can receive a **1-ounce trial-size packet** good for two to four uses. Plus, you receive a buy-one-get-one-free coupon on a future purchase.

Just the Dirt, Ma'am

SEND:
$2 P&H

ASK FOR:
Three Samples of Skin Care Products

MAIL TO:
**Lite-Cosmetics
2124 El Camino Real, #201
Oceanside, CA 92054**

Most soaps have a pH level much higher than the natural pH level of our skin. They strip away the dirt but also remove your skin's own protective oils. Lite-Cosmetics® has created cleansers that leave the skin's natural moisture levels intact. With this offer you'll get **three samples of new, natural products from Lite-Cosmetics®.** You'll receive Evening Magic®, a rich night cream containing natural proteins and vitamins with aromatherapy; Eye and Throat Creme, made with natural carrot oil to reduce the appearance of fine lines in these age-prone areas; and Hand and Body Lotion, which has a silky, nongreasy feeling.

Nail Care by Mail

Realys Incorporated has supplied professional manicurists for over 10 years. Now they want to put the best nail tools right in your hands. Send for your **FREE**

SEND:

A long SASE

ASK FOR:

**Realys® Washable
Nail File**

MAIL TO:

**Realys Professional
Nail Care
7601 Woodwind Dr.
Huntington Beach, CA
92647**

Realys® washable nail file from their new line of professional quality products for consumers.

Unsightly Toenails?

SEND:

$2 P&H

ASK FOR:

**Sample Tube of Fungal
Nail Revitalizer**

MAIL TO:

**Footsmart Products
507-B Maple Leaf Dr.
Dept 18
Nashville, TN 37210**

Do you suffer from discolored, thickened toenails caused by fungal nail infections? Podiatrist's Secret® **Fungal Nail Revitalizer** helps bring back the natural look and feel of healthy toenails. This mildly abrasive cream gently reduces discoloration and smooths out rough, scaly nails.

Fungal Nail Revitalizer normally sells for $6.95, but for a small shipping and handling fee you can try a full ounce of this foot cream. A nail brush is also included. In just a few days your feet will look better and feel better, with fewer worries about unsightly toenails.

HEALTH, FITNESS, AND NUTRITION

Be Sure with BreathAsure®

SEND:
A long SASE

ASK FOR:
**Single-Use Pack
of BreathAsure
(Limit 1 per household)**

MAIL TO:
**BreathAsure, Dept. SUP
26115 Mureau Rd.
Calabasas, CA
91302-3126**

BreathAsure® is a unique breath freshener that works internally with your digestive system—the source of bad breath. This 100 percent natural product fights bad breath associated with garlic, onions, and other odors. It even fights morning breath.

Send for a **FREE single use packet of BreathAsure®.** It is a unique blend of parsley seed and sunflower oil in a soft capsule. It contains no artificial flavors, colors, preservatives, alcohol, or sugar. And, unlike mints, gum, or mouthwash, it doesn't mask bad breath, it eliminates it!

Confidence in a Capsule

PHONE:
1-800-688-3933

ASK FOR:
BeSure Capsules

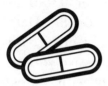

Attention, ladies and gentlemen! Now you can eat beans and vegetables with the confidence of knowing that you won't experience embarrassing flatulence. Request this FREE offer from the makers of **BeSure Capsules.**

Taking a capsule before eating will eliminate intestinal gas before it starts. The product is allergy-safe and is effective with both hot and cold foods. The makers have set up a toll-free telephone number so that you can call right away for this FREE sample offer.

Diabetes Telephone Directory

SEND:
A long SASE

ASK FOR:
**LifeScan
Tele-Library Card**

MAIL TO:
**LifeScan
Tele-Library Card
485 Madison Ave.,
4th Floor
New York, NY 10022**

Diabetes is not a rare condition. It afflicts about 14 million Americans. If you are diabetic, you should have up-to-date information. LifeScan provides prerecorded information on a variety of diabetes topics 24 hours a day, and a **FREE Tele-Library card** will allow you to access this service.

Getting Creative with Dates

PHONE:
1-800-223-8748

ASK FOR:
Date Recipes

California Dates, nature's delicious, portable snack for today's life on the go. Dates are high in fiber and potassium and are free of sodium, fat, and cholesterol. Good nutrition never tasted so great! The California Date Administration is offering you FREE recipes to assist you in cooking creatively with dates. The recipes range from desserts to dinners. With a little imagination, this simple fruit can add a delicious twist to an endless variety of recipes. Call for your **FREE recipes** now and start cooking!

Hug Crazy

SEND:
A large SASE

ASK FOR:
Let's Hug

MAIL TO:

**Once Upon A Planet
39 Norwood Rd.
Port Washington, N Y
11050**

Let's Hug is a **FREE two-page newsletter** that encourages everyone to become Hug Initiators. So dedicated is the publisher that when you request information you'll also get a little stack of colorful Hug Coupons to pass along to others, thus expanding the hug movement across the country.

Miracle Worker

Your face may feel clean after you wash it, but the top layer may still have dead skin, which can clog pores, prevent moisturizers from penetrating, and make fine lines appear larger. Unlike scrubs or loofah sponges, which can cause microscopic tears in the skin, the Beautiful Skin Kit gently removes dull, dead skin. You can receive a **FREE ½-ounce sample of skin cream** and detailed directions for proper use. Dermatologists have dubbed the cream, "miracle in a jar." Try it and be on your way to younger, healthier skin!

It's a Quiet Diet

Now you can make healthy food choices and maintain all the benefits of fiber without the uncomfortable side effects. Beano, a dietary supplement, contains a natural food enzyme that improves the digestibility of "gassy" foods such as broccoli, cabbage, beans, and whole grain cereals and bread.

Send for a **FREE sample of Beano tablets.** You will also receive money-saving coupons good toward your next store purchase.

100-Mile Dash

SEND:
A long SASE

ASK FOR:
100 Mile Club packet

MAIL TO:
**U.S. 100 Mile Club
P.O. Box 1208
Alturas, CA 96101-1208**

Respond to a physical challenge—join the **100 Mile Club.** The club promotes exercise by asking members to take a pledge to complete "100 Miles of Exercise." It can be any kind of exercise, and one mile is credited for every 10 minutes of activity such as walking, aerobics, and biking.

If you're motivated to get fit and have fun doing it, send for this FREE club membership.

Pamper Your Feet

SEND:
$2 P&H

ASK FOR:
**Sample Pair of
Feet Pleasers™
Specify: shoe size**

MAIL TO:
**Footsmart Products
507-B Maple Leaf Dr.
Dept 18
Nashville, TN 37210**

Women, pamper your feet all day with **Feet Pleasers™.** These amazingly thin soles provide protection from foot shock impact and give all-day comfort. The ¾ shoe-length design won't cramp or crowd your toes and is perfect for those favorite flats or heels.

These insoles regularly sell for $4.95, but now you can try a pair of Feet Pleasers™ for just a small shipping and handling fee. Constructed from Enduron™ foam material, Feet Pleasers™ absorb "step shock impact" to prevent tired, aching feet and legs.

Wonder Feet

SEND:
$2 P&H

ASK FOR:
**Sample pair of
Wonder Walkers
Specify: women's or
men's and shoe size**

MAIL TO:
**Footsmart Products
507-B Maple Leaf Dr.
Dept. 18
Nashville, TN 37210**

Wonder Walkers® are a godsend for people who live and work on their feet. These high-performance insole liners provide the ultimate combination of shock protection and cushioning comfort and durability.

These insoles regularly sell for $5.95, but now you can try a **pair of Wonder Walkers®** for just a small shipping fee. Constructed of a new foam material, Wonder Walkers® have benefits not only for your feet but also for your legs, knees, and back. And they last long, retaining over 95 percent of their original cushioning even after hundreds of miles.

Workout Wallet

SEND:
$1.75 P&H

ASK FOR:
Workout Wallet

MAIL TO:
**Neetstuf
Dept. FR-97
P.O. Box 353
Rio Grande, NJ 08242**

Picture this: It's time for your first aerobics class and you want to take some money along, just in case you decide to make a break for the juice bar. You don't want to leave the house unlocked, so you need to take your key. But your new workout suit doesn't have pockets. What do you do? Send for the **workout wallet,** which wraps around your wrist. The lightweight wallet is made of waterproof vinyl, and the attached Velcro keeps it secure on your wrist. It's thin enough to be comfortable, but wide enough to hold money and keys. You'll be off to aerobics and feeling great with nothing but your new workout wallet secured to your wrist and a smile on your face.

PERSONAL SAFETY

Playing It Safe

SEND:
$1.75 P&H

ASK FOR:
Hidden Wallet

MAIL TO:
**Neetstuf, FR-90
P.O. Box 353
Rio Grande, NJ 08242**

We lock our houses and apartments because we want to keep our money and valuables safe. But when you're traveling or out shopping, you should take similar precautions when you're carrying money with you. You can keep your money safer by using the **hidden wallet.** This sturdy, lightweight, waterproof vinyl wallet hangs over your neck and stays hidden under your jacket or sweater. It has two zippered pockets big enough for your money, credit cards, keys, and other small items.

PETS

Are You Curious about Cats?

If you love cats, you won't be able to keep your paws off this **sample issue of *CATS*** magazine. This full-color glossy is America's oldest cat publication featuring news about felines and their fascinating lives. Curious cat owners who check out this magazine will find advice columns, book reviews, and health information.

There's also lots of reader anecdotes, crafts, cat comics, and even a regular section that gives readers the chance to have photos of their favorite cats published.

Brush Up

Dogs and cats love a gentle stroke across their fur. And what better way to give your pet some attention than by brushing its coat to keep it clean, smooth,

SEND:
$1.75 P&H

ASK FOR:
Pet Brush

MAIL TO:
**Jaye Products, Inc.
Dept. 14
P.O. Box 10726
Naples, FL 33941**

and free of fleas. This **self-cleaning pet brush** is the perfect tool for grooming. The three-inch-round plastic brush fits comfortably in the palm of your hand. It has soft bristles that massage your pet's skin and retract with a twist of your hand to easily remove matted hair.

Hail to the Cat

SEND:
A long SASE

ASK FOR:
Sample issue of
Socks the Cat Fan Club Newsletter

MAIL TO:
**Socks the Cat Fan Club
611 South Ivy St.
Arlington, VA 22204**

No matter where President Clinton's popularity is in the polls, affection for his cat, Socks, America's first "DemoCat" in the White House, is at an all-time high. If you are a fan of the First Feline or just a regular cat fan, send for a **FREE sample issue of** *Socks the Cat Fan Club Newsletter* **and a photo of Socks.**

A recent issue of this eight-page newsletter featured a letter from Socks, children's poetry and drawings, and educational articles on how a bill becomes a law.

I Love My Pet

SEND:
Your name and address and one loose first-class stamp

ASK FOR:
FREE issue of
The Pet Club Gazette

MAIL TO:
Spectrum Business Services
231 E. Alessandro Blvd.
Suite A-158
Dept. F
Riverside, CA 92508

If you love your pet, here's a terrific **FREE newsletter** just for you. *The Pet Club Gazette* is a monthly newsletter written just for pet lovers. Each issue is packed with valuable information on grooming, health, training, and enjoying your pet. There's also a pen-pal exchange, helpful hints, and much, much more to help you take good care of your pet.

Pets and Apartments

SEND:
$1

ASK FOR:
"Pets in People Places"

MAIL TO:
Massachusetts SPCA
350 S. Huntington Ave.
Boston, MA 02130

Many apartment owners do not allow you to have a pet. Usually, once you sign a "no pet" clause lease you have no recourse. Sometimes conflicts occur between landlord and tenant even when pets are allowed. Apartment owners and dwellers can get guidelines to help work out any differences. Send for "Pets in People Places."

Snap to It

SEND:
$2 P&H

ASK FOR:
Cat Snaps® Treats

MAIL TO:
Prime Pet Products
P.O. Box 2473
Beverly Hills, CA 90213

Pleasing your cat is a snap with a sample **box of Cat Snaps®**. Your favorite feline won't be able to resist these flavor-filled tablet treats. Cat Snaps® help keep your cat or kitten in good health with a glossy coat. They contain natural vitamins and minerals usually not found in regular pet food. This 90-tablet supply is enough for two to six weeks.

PRIZES AND GIVEAWAYS

Read 'em and Sweep

SEND:
A long SASE

ASK FOR:
Sample copy of
Sweeping the USA

MAIL TO:
Delosh
171 Water St.
Massena, NY 13662

Sweepstakes and contests offer exciting opportunities to win valuable prizes and money while playing in the comfort of your own home. Literally thousands of prizes are given away every month by major companies.

Learn more about how you can increase your odds of being in the money with a **FREE sample issue** of *Sweeping the USA,* a four-page newsletter that includes winning tips, ideas, and up-to-date sources of national sweepstakes.

Sweep Success

Find out how you can enter hundreds of contests and sweepstakes by getting a **FREE sample issue of** *Best Sweepstakes Newsletter.* Thousands of lucky people win huge sums of cash and big prizes

SEND:
A long SASE with two first class stamps affixed

ASK FOR:
Sample copy of
Best Sweepstakes Newsletter
and
Best Extra

MAIL TO:
BSN
4215 Winnetka Ave. N.
Suite 219
New Hope, MN 55428

through corporate-sponsored sweepstakes.

Every month, this 12-page newsletter publishes details on approximately 30 current contests. It also contains interesting editorials, tips, and reader comments. As an added bonus you'll receive a **FREE sample issue of** *Best Extra,* a new four-page supplemental bulletin that features short running sweepstakes.

Take Your Cuts

SEND:
$1 P&H (postage stamps accepted)

ASK FOR:
Issue of *Refundle Bundle*

MAIL TO:
Select Coupon Club
Box 338-FB
Tuckahoe, NY 10707

Learn from *Family Circle*'s refund and coupon expert Susan Samtur with a copy of her national publication *Refundle Bundle.*

Refundle Bundle is a monthly 48-page refund and coupon guide containing more than 400 offers made by virtually every manufacturer conceivable. The publication also reports on consumer news such as recalls, product introductions, and tips and ideas contributed by readers.

SPORTS AND RECREATION

Animal Attraction

SEND:
$2 P&H

ASK FOR:
**Football Team Magnet
(indicate favorite
National Football
League team)**

MAIL TO:
**Neetstuf Dept. FM-1
P.O. Box 353
Rio Grande, NJ 08242**

If you're wild about football, you'll go bonkers for this **Tasmanian Devil NFL Team Magnet.** This 2-inch-tall rubberized magnet features the crazy Taz equipped in his football gear with a banner bearing the name of your favorite team. Taz has a different pose for each of your favorite teams. Let Taz help you when it's third down and long yardage.

A Giant Offer

The National Football Conference East has long been regarded one of the toughest divisions in the pro game. The teams have a reputation for playing an old-school brand of smash-mouth football, and the New York Giants are arguably the best at it.

SEND:
$1 P&H

ASK FOR:
Sample Issue of
The Giants Newsweekly

MAIL TO:
The Giants Newsweekly
P.O. Box 816
Red Bank, NJ 07701

If you are a Giants fan or simply a giant football fan, you'll want to send for a **sample issue of** ***The Giants Newsweekly.*** This tabloid-size newspaper covers all the news that's Giants news— player profiles, interviews, stats, predictions, commentary, and more. Usually sold for $2.50 an issue, a sample copy is yours for only one dollar.

Fun for the Road

SEND:
$1 P&H

ASK FOR:
Plastic Checker Set

MAIL TO:
Just For Fun
Dept. 207
P.O. Box 509
Pottsville, PA 17901

"Are we there yet?" Those are the famous first words of young travelers everywhere who can't wait to arrive at that vacation destination. To help pass the time, no family trip should be without a travel game. And this **mini plastic checker set** is perfect for those long car trips. The paper board is 6 by 6 inches and comes with one set of plastic mini checkers in black and red.

It's in the Clouds

SEND:
$1 P&H

ASK FOR:
"How to Forecast the Weather" Booklet

MAIL TO:
Cloud Chart Inc.
P.O. Box 21298
Charleston, SC 29413

A change in the weather seldom comes as a surprise to those who recognize nature's signals. If you are interested in a scientific approach to weather predicting, send for this **pocket guide on "How to Forecast the Weather."**

This 10-page booklet gives information on foretelling the weather based on clouds and presents full-color photos of various sky patterns. It also offers interesting facts on wind and lightning.

Stick with Your Team

SEND:
$1.25 P&H

ASK FOR:
Baseball Team Logo Stickers (indicate favorite team)

MAIL TO:
Mr. Rainbows
Dept. FK-14
P.O. Box 908
Rio Grande, NJ 08242

When the words "Batter Up" echo throughout the stadium, you'll want to show off your favorite team by decorating your room or notebook with these **officially licensed Major League Baseball logo stickers.** You get a 7- by 7-inch sheet that contains 10 stickers in various sizes featuring the logo of your favorite team. Just be sure to let the supplier know what team you root for.

Stuck in the Craw

SEND:
$1 P&H for one, or $2 for three

ASK FOR:
Cajun Crawfish Lure

MAIL TO:
**Ol' John's Lures
7979 Hwy. 3015
Keatchie, LA 71046**

All streams, rivers, and other bodies of water in the United States have live crawfish . . . and fish love 'em. As a sport fisherman, you can take advantage of this fact by getting the hot-blooded **Cajun Crawfish fishing lure.**

Great for crappie, white perch, speckled perch, bream, trout, bass, and other game fish, the Cajun Crawfish works with light tackle. No pinch-on weight is needed; it's molded right into the lure's head. Use it just like live bait, with or without a float.

THINGS FOR THE GRANDKIDS

Forest Friends Fun Pack

SEND:
Your name and address

ASK FOR:
**Junior Forest Ranger Kit
or Woodsy Fan Mail Pack**

FOR **Smokey Bear,**
MAIL TO:
**Smokey Bear
Headquarters
P.O. Box 1963
Washington, DC 20252**

FOR **Woodsy Owl,**
MAIL TO:
**Woodsy Owl Fan Mail
P.O. Box 1963
Washington, DC 20252**

Here are two new friends you will want a favorite youngster to meet: Smokey Bear and Woodsy Owl. Write to Woodsy or Smokey and they will send you a FREE fun pack with ideas and activity lists showing what you can do to help preserve our planet. Smokey offers a **FREE Junior Forest Ranger Kit** with activities, membership card, and badge. Woodsy sends a **FREE fan mail pack** with activities, songs, and pictures to color.

Grandparent Times

Here's something to bring grandparents and their grandchildren closer together. *Grandparent Times* offers grandparents "many ways to cultivate and nurture the fruits of the imagination—both your

SEND:
$1 P&H

ASK FOR:
Sample Issue of
Grandparent Times

MAIL TO:
Caring Grandparents
of America
400 Seventh St., NW,
Suite 302
Washington, DC
20004-2206

own and your grandchildren's." The newsletter is printed in full color and includes information on benefits and savings for seniors, delicious and cost-cutting recipes, and answers to frequently asked questions.

Recreational Reading

SEND:
$1.50 P&H

ASK FOR:
Magazine of your choice

MAIL TO:
CBHI
1100 Waterway Blvd.
Indianapolis, IN 46202

Are you looking for a way to get a young child interested in reading? If so, then it's time you were introduced to some of the best **children's magazines.** Choose *Children's Digest, Turtle Magazine for Preschool Kids, Humpty Dumpty's Magazine, Children's Playmate Magazine, Jack and Jill,* or *Child Life.*

Some Enchanted Evening

"Peter Pan," "The Jungle Book," "Cinderella," and "Pinocchio" are some of the best loved classics of children's literature. Kids, parents, and grandparents know these stories through their animated film adaptations. The **"Enchanted Tales" storybooks,** however, offer the opportunity to start young children on the active journey of reading.

There are a variety of titles available, including the aforementioned stories (supplier's choice). Each softcover book is 16 pages long with color illustrations.

INDEX